Inspired By Love

Helen Thwaites

Inspired By Love

Published by Woodlark Publishing
Copyright © Helen Thwaites
ISBN-13: 9780993349164
ISBN-10: 0993349161

All rights reserved.
The moral right of the author has been asserted.
No part of this publication may be reproduced, stored in a retrieval system, or transmitted in any form or by any means, without the prior consent of the author, nor be otherwise circulated in any form of binding or cover other than that in which it is published and without a similar condition being imposed on the subsequent purchaser.

Inspired By Love

Seasons

Inspired By Love

<u>New Beginnings</u>

New Year, new start and
Expectations high,
With goals to achieve,
Bringing fulfilment and joy.
Every new experience
Giving purpose
In our lives.
Nature's beauty
Now gradually awakes,
Inspiring us to go and explore.
No stone left unturned, or
Gateway ignored,
So let us move forward with hope and good cheer.

Inspired By Love

A New Year

As we embark on this New Year,
May we learn to live by your truth,
May all our thoughts be filled with love,
May all our deeds be done with mercy,
May all our words be spoken with grace,
And may we keep you at the centre,
Hour by hour,
Day by day,
Week by week,
And month by month,
As we live our lives,
And throughout the year.

Changes

Changing scenes,
Different colours,
Signalling each season,
All are appealing,
Each one unique,
For all there is a reason.

Inspired By Love

Seasons

Each season lives,
Each season dies,
Each season has its lows and highs,
Spring and summer, autumn, winter,
Each has charm and always alters,
Not one day the same;

Spring brings new life,
Spring gives us hope,
Spring time enables us to cope,
Easter time brings gladness to spring,
Young animals and birds bring joy,
Time to start afresh;

Summer means warmth,
Summer means sun,
Summertime for children means fun,
Trips to the beach and holidays,
Days out to learn and to enjoy,
A great time for all;

Inspired By Love

Autumn brings change,
Autumn means flight,
Autumn time makes a lovely sight,
Leaves change colour and birds migrate,
Harvest time provides food for all,
Ever changing scenes;

Winter brings cold,
Winter is dark,
Winter time makes the land look stark,
Days are so short and nights so black,
The snow and ice can make life hard,
But the earth is cleaned;

Each season lives,
Each season dies,
Each season has its lows and highs,
Each brings us gifts throughout the year,
We do not always see or hear,
But each one will come.

Inspired By Love

Changing Seasons

The flowers of summer fade and fall,
The trees take on their autumn hues,
We long for spring time's cuckoo's call,
To chase away the winter blues.

Our summer visitors take their flight,
Autumns fruits are ready to eat,
Spring's new life is a joyous sight,
Christmas is a reason to meet.

The warmth of summer and days of fun,
Give way to autumn's misty haze,
New born lambs gambol in the sun,
As winter melts, as in a daze.

Charm exists in every season,
And for each there is a reason.

Inspired By Love

A Valentines Thought

Chocolates or roses,
What shall it be?
Valentine's Day is special you see.
A day to be thankful,
For friendship that's true,
And not take for granted,
People like you.
Our greatest of gifts,
Are the people we love,
Whether they're down here with us,
Or looking on from above.
We know in our hearts,
And can never forget,
The love that we share is always enough.

Spring Heralds

Pure and white snowdrops,
Subtle yellow primroses,
Bloom to herald spring,
Bringing the hoped for promise,
That better times are ahead.

Inspired By Love

<u>The perfect spring</u>

A walk along a country lane,
Brings joy and peace and calm,
Countryside so wonderful,
An outlook so serene,
The bird song fills you full of glee,
The flowers full of hope,
Spring sunshine fills you full of warmth,
New life brings so much fun,
To breath the clear fresh air so sweet,
Makes you feel so full of life,
The season of spring brings so much cheer,
And happiness all around;

The breezes rustle all the leaves,
So new and fresh and green,
A lush green meadow full of life,
A clear spring sky so blue,
The butterflies are full of charm,
The hedgerows full of bloom,
Spring colours and the sounds so strong,
Young animals at play,
They skip and run and jump and hop,
Through pastures wide and free and green,
They will gamble the whole day long.

Inspired By Love

Spring Cleaning

Soap suds and scrubbing brush,
Polish and paint tins,
Racing around in a terrible rush;

I empty all the bins,
Now to wash the floors,
Got so much to do, my head it just spins;

Cleaning windows and doors,
Letting in the light,
Eradicating all unwanted spores;

A continuing fight,
Not one I can lose,
It's always such a discouraging sight;

Never a job I choose,
Gleeful when it's done,
The vacuum must work and not blow a fuse;

How do I make this fun?
Outside and inside,
Unblock the drains or lay out in the sun?

Grateful and full of pride,
Happy all looks plush,
Thankful all is done with joy now I stride.

Inspired By Love

Spring Green

Spring is green and lush and new,
With verdant greens of every hue,
Hues that dance and hues that calm,
Some that sing, others that whisper,
Shades that sparkle, shades that gleam,
And many others in between.

Blue-black hues that loom and lower,
Rich deep greens bring strength and power,
Silvery shades as though frost-encrusted,
Shadowy shades that are not quite trusted,
Spring is green and lush and new,
Thank you spring for being you.

Easter

Everlasting father
Always there for me,
Sacrificed to pay my debt
That I might be set free,
Every day I thank you
Remembering the cost.

Inspired By Love

An Easter thought

As we celebrate this Easter,
Let's remember what it means,
That Jesus Christ should die for us,
So we may be redeemed;

God sent his one and only son,
To die at Calvary,
To forgive our sins so we can live,
With him eternally;

By his blood we can be cleansed,
And healed by his power,
Our faith grows stronger everyday,
Through living by his word;

Our hope comes from his resurrection,
Bringing light into this world,
Trust in him with all your heart,
And he will bring you through.

Inspired By Love

A gift of love

On that day you gave your life,
You died to set me free,
Your arms of love were open wide,
To show your love for me;

You took my pain and all my sin,
That day at Calvary,
On the cross you paid the price,
So I could be forgiven;

You rose again, you gave me hope,
You brought light into the world,
From that day on you led the way,
Your glory was unfurled;

When you ascended into heaven,
You gave us such a gift,
You sent to us your Holy Spirit,
To be forever here.

Inspired By Love

Christ's sacrifice

The selfless love of Jesus,
Displayed upon a cross,
The sinless Saviour crucified,
To pay the debt for us.

Summer Nymph

Afflatus comes but once a year,
A sign of hope that brings good cheer,
At dead of night she skips and plays,
Through all the streets and alley ways,
When morning breaks she has gone again,
But her work is done and will remain
Until the autumn wind and rain.

Inspired By Love

Harvest

A time for reaping the seeds that we've sown,
A time to gather the fruit which has grown.

Through long summer days the fields have turned gold,
We harvest them all before it turns cold.

The fruit on the trees and bushes are ripe,
So they are picked and boxed and sold by type.

Fishermen harvest their crop all year round,
Not spending long with their feet on dry ground.

From nectar they gather, bees make honey,
When put into jars we can make money.

Harvest describes a time of collection,
Time to look back, a time for reflection.

Of work which is done throughout the whole year,
And culminates with a time of good cheer.

Inspired By Love

Autumn

Crowns of gold and gowns of green,
Reds, browns and yellows in between,
Leaves which adorn tall statues of trees,
Standing bejewelled in autumn's scene;

Shiny plump blackberries ripe for the picking,
Onions and beetroot ready for pickling,
Hedgerows of berries providing a feast,
For birds and for beasts as the year's clock is ticking;

Days getting shorter with a chill in the air,
Dewdrops that cling to silk finer than hair,
But when woven together they form a trap,
Giving food to the spider who hides in his lair;

The harvest all safely gathered and stored,
The fruit of the vine into bottles is poured,
The smell of preserving escapes from the kitchen,
Chutneys and jams once made adored;

Inspired By Love

When autumn arrives, winter soon follows;
And creatures will hibernate in hedgerows and hollows,
But do not despair or give up your hope,
For when winter is done and heralds in spring,
From far away shores come the swifts and the swallows.

Autumn Haiku

Leaves crunch under foot,
The breeze whispers through the trees,
Feathers at your feet.

Natural Treasures

Intricately laced with finest silken thread,
Is how a spider weaves its web,
The beauty of these structures,
Is there for all to see,
In the early winter mornings,
They glisten white with frost,
And in the autumn, spring and summer,
They shimmer with crystal drops of dew.

Inspired By Love

A view of winter weather

To see the snowflakes falling,
It's like watching tiny ballerinas dance,
Each one unique, individual and different,
All with grace, elegance and charm,
They land so gently on the earth,
And create a different scene;

The snow brings fun for children,
Some will make a snowman some have snowball for fights,
Like a snowflake each child has charm and is unique,
So all have fun in their own way,
They all use snow so differently,
That fantasy can come true;

Inspired By Love

Snow also causes danger,
Both vehicles and pedestrians can suffer,
Pedestrians may fall and cars could slip and crash,
Many people are hurt like this,
On occasions it is fatal,
Sometimes through stupidity;

There's nothing wrong with having fun in the winter weather,
But just make sure what's fun for you isn't harmful to another.

Daybreak

Early morning sun,
Trimming clouds with golden light,
Starts a winter day.

Snow 1

Lacy white crystals,
Dancing like ballerinas,
A blanket appears.

Inspired By Love

Snow 2

Crystals of white lace,
Dancing ballerinas fall,
Blanketing the earth.

Winter Crystals

Crystals of the frost,
The chill tendrils of winter,
Herald nature's sleep.

Winter Warmth

A hearty warm meal,
Can satisfy and comfort,
Throughout winter's gloom.

Inspired By Love

Art and Nature

Early on a winter morn,
With frost upon the ground,
A spider's web is glistening,
In the light from winter's sun.
Encrusted with white, it shimmers,
As though laden with diamonds and crystal.
This finely woven work of art,
Puts joy into my heart.

A Christmas thought

Christmas is a time for joy, goodwill, hope, love and fun,
A time for all the family and children most of all,
A time for giving and receiving many cards and gifts,
We all eat and we all drink a plentiful and tasty fayre,
Most people take all this for granted,
They do not spare a single thought for those less fortunate,
But many children and their families will never know all this;

Inspired By Love

It's people such as these that need our thoughts and prayers,
If only we would think of them and share our Christmas fun,
But not to turn our backs on them when yuletide is done;

Christmas should be free to all but this is not the case,
For those who suffer from abuse, depravity and hate,
The poor, the needy, sick and hungry have no Christmas time,
They do not eat and they do not drink, they have no lavish feast,
These people can celebrate nothing,
Why could we not be less selfish and share this festive time,
Let's make Christmas time come true for all children and their families;

Buy an extra gift or cook an extra meal,
Open your house, invite them in and make them feel welcome,
Please share with them as Jesus did what Christmas really means.

Inspired By Love

Christmas

Christian
Hearts
Renewed
In
Strength
Through
Mankind's
Amazing
Saviour.

Christmas

The children singing carols all across the land,
Round every single corner we see a merry band,
There's people buying presents,
And others buying food,
Everyone we meet seems to be in festive mood;

There's a display in every window,
And lights for all to see;

Inspired By Love

In every Christmas grotto there's a child on Santa's knee,
Telling him the gift they want to find beneath their tree,
Grand parties are attended,
Grand banquets are prepared,
Families unite this season for a happy time that's shared.

Christmas Verses

Christ was born at Christmas,
Bringing light into our world,
So may your celebrations,
Be filled with the joy of our Lord.

Brightly coloured baubles hanging on the tree,
Presents for the girls and boys are there for all to see,
A time for celebration and sharing festive cheer,
But don't forget our Saviour born on Christmas Day.

Inspired By Love

Christmas comes but once a year,
To fill our lives with fun and good cheer,
So this greeting comes to you,
To bless you and let you know you are loved,
Now and the whole year through.

As you celebrate this Christmas,
May you feel the love and blessing,
That comes with this simple greeting,
From me and our Saviour above.

This simple Christmas greeting,
Comes from me to you,
Wishing you peace and happiness,
Now and the whole year through.

Inspired By Love

The weather

Throughout the year the weather changes,
Hot summer sun,
Encouraging fun,
Windy autumn days,
Emptying the trees of their jewel coloured leaves,
And in the depth of winter,
The snow thick on the ground,
Happy Christmas to everyone,
Enjoy this time of cheer,
Remember spring with its new start is just around the corner.

Inspired By Love

Weather through the seasons

In winter's grip the world lies asleep,
Under blankets of snow and crystallised frost.
With its biting winds and bitter cold,
How long will this go on?
The icy grip begins to fade,
And signs of spring appear.
We still wake to crystallised frost on the lawn,
But the warming sun and gentler winds,
Send it quickly on its way.
April showers are not much fun,
But having fed the earth will soon be passed.
The sun gets stronger the heat increases,
Spring glides into summer.
With its long hot days and occasional storms,
When thunder and lightening perform,
Providing rain which we need but do not want,
To refresh the ground again.
The winds of autumn herald change,
Bringing mists and morning dew,
We still get some sun but less sultry heat,
The leaves of the trees change colour and fall.
Gales appear meaning winter is near,
The weather goes full circle each year.

Inspired By Love

Unseen Power

How can I smell salt on the air?
When no sea is to be found?
How do birds glide?
Their wings so unmoving,
Why is a feather blowing against my cheek?
Feeling like a heavenly kiss,
What is this unknown phenomenon?
Something so unheard and unseen,
With power in silence and without form,
That can stir the leaves from silent slumber,
What can it be?
But it is the wind.

Inspired By Love

<u>What Threatens?</u>

The sky grey and sinister,
Heralding what is to come,
From behind me things begin to change,
First the twigs begin to twitch,
Before the birds of the air begin to pitch,
Swooping to earth falling lower and lower,
Before being caught and hurled back aloft.
Caught in a power unseen and unheard,
A frolicsome gust,
A billowing breeze,
Playful and powerful,
Enemy or friend,
The wind is unknown, untamed but believed.

Inspired By Love

<u>Grey Sky</u>

A leaden grey sky,
Lowering and ominous,
Oppressiveness waits.

<u>Wind</u>

A gusty wind blows,
The rumble down the chimney,
Hollow, eerie sounds.

Inspired By Love

Invisible Strength

Carried high,
Carried above,
What is this thing which lifts the dove?

Flat to the ground,
Beaten and blown,
What flattens the reeds that so tall had grown?

Creaks and groans,
Whimpers and moans,
What rattles the frame of the place I call home?

Chilling the air,
Swirling around,
Picking things up and putting them down?

Standing in awe,
Watching a show,
Put on by nothing, nothing more than the wind.

Inspired By Love

With Every Single Breath

With every single breath of wind,
A change is taking place,
The scene around us alters,
Above our heads and at our feet,
Clouds change light and shadows,
As they scamper in the wind,
Leaves and twigs and other treasures,
Scatter on the breeze.
As with the heavenly breath of God,
Whose touch throughout our lives,
Heralds different seasons,
Different chapters in our lives,
Comfort when in sorrow,
Healing when in pain,
Every breath from God above,
Brings forth a brand new day.

Inspired By Love

The winds of change

In the icy blast of winter,
You are biting, cruel and cold,
Bringing with you snowfall,
Earth is frozen hard as stone.

In the warming air of spring time,
You gently thaw the frozen ground,
Bringing forth a new start,
And hope to move us forward.

In the heat and sun of summer,
Your breath comes as a cooling breeze,
Bringing with you pleasure,
Seaside trips and holidays.

In the cooler air of autumn,
You herald yet another time,
Bringing jewel colours,
To leaves on shrubs and trees.

So throughout the year and seasons,
You have a vital role to play,
Bringing change and newness,
We say thank you to the wind.

Inspired By Love

Places

Inspired By Love

<u>Beccles</u>

Boat trips on the river,
Excellent places to eat,
Countryside on your doorstep,
Creative, cultural pastimes,
Loving friendships,
Easily found,
So thank you Beccles for being my home.

Inspired By Love

Beccles Open Gardens

Blossoms
Exquisitely
Creating
Calm
Lifting
Each
Spirit
Of
People
Entering.
Naturally
Growing
And
Regally
Dressed
Exhibiting
Natures
Success.
All
Neatly
Designed
Showing
Perfect
Adornment
Capturing
Every
Sense.

Inspired By Love

Beccles Charter Weekend

Bringing
Excitement,
Creating
Cheer,
Linking
Events,
Sharing
Community
History.
Art
Reaching
To
Everyone,
Revealing
With
Ease,
Each
Kind
Encouraging
New
Dreams.

Inspired By Love

Beccles Area River Cavalcade

Boats
Enhance
Charter
Celebrations,
Letting
Explorers
See
Amazing
Riverside
Establishments,
And
Rejoice
In
Various
Events
River
Centred,
Allowing
Visitors
And
Locals
Combined,
Amazing
Days of
Excitement.

Inspired By Love

The River

Two counties divided,
Yet united by a river,
That meanders through countryside, village and town,
Until at its end it reaches the sea.

Traffic and industry,
Thunders over and around it.
Bridges and factories, office blocks and high-rise flats,
Hard, cold and unyielding.

Pumping out emissions,
And choking nature's breath,
Destroying for profit,
Consideration and respect sadly lacking.

Further along its winding path,
This gentle vein of flowing water,
Leaves the ugly world of business and industry behind,
Drawing you into the peace and tranquillity,
Of lush green meadows and marshes.

Inspired By Love

The air here carries a sweeter fragrance,
One of blossoms and ripening fruit.
Birdsong and the rustling of leaves,
Replace the traffic's roar,
Before itself being replaced by noises of the farmyard.

Clucks and neighing,
Barks and braying,
A different music now fills the air.
The fragrances here are different too,
Maybe some not so sweet,
But natural and far less offensive than where the river began.

You can taste home cooked food from an open back door,
As the river leads from wild to wild to wild.
Now again a different flavour hangs in a different wind.
Salt is the flavour,
Coupled with smoke from the smoke house,
And the catch of the day.

Inspired By Love

The freshwater river now joins the sea,
Where its power is greatly increased.
The bird calls filling your ears at this final point,
Are harsher than earlier on,
As the gulls swoop and dive,
The river is alive as it runs,
To the embrace of the sea.

Southwold

Salt flavours the air,
Odour of hops,
Ugly power station on the far horizon,
The pebbles become sand beneath my feet,
Hot sun beating down,
Waves musically ebb and flow,
Over pebbles and sand,
Laughing children all around,
Daydreaming summer days.

Inspired By Love

Assembled

Theatrical
Heartfelt
Exuberance
Artistically
Serenade
Society.
Exquisite
Marriages
Bless
Lovers
Yearly.
Historical
Orators
Uncover
Secrets
Educating
Norfolk.
Opulence,
Richness,
Wealthy
Increasingly
Cavort
Here.

Inspired By Love

The Lake District

This
Haven of
England, with it's
Lakes providing peace,
And mountains to climb.
Keswick and Kendal are there to
Explore.
Derwent water
Is easily found.
Stone circles in fields and
Tea shops in towns.
Reflect and
Imagine,
Create what you will,
There is something for all to enjoy.

Inspired By Love

Blencathra

A view from every window,
So peaceful and serene,
A blessing every morning,
Each day a changing scene;

The sheep out in the field,
The dramatic mountain peaks,
The memories which we yield,
Are different for each one;

The Lord made his creation,
So wherever we may roam,
In any land or nation,
We may feel we're coming home.

Inspired By Love

Blencathra

Beautiful views
Lay in the valley,
Every minute a changing scene.
Nature is abundant,
Capturing imagination
Animals and landscape
Tell their own story.
Haven of peace
Reflecting God's
Awesome power.

Northward bound

The journey north takes a long time,
But the views that await us are so worthwhile,
The imposing mountains and lakes sublime;
The journey north takes a long time,
Revealing natures beauty in her prime,
Every aspect makes me smile;
The journey north takes a long time,
But the views that await us are so worthwhile.

Inspired By Love

The holiday

With great anticipation we set out on the road,
The road that takes us northwards,
To share a holiday with friends,
A time to go exploring the stunning country side,
A landscape very different from the one we left behind.

The challenges of each new day differ for each one,
Gently walking round a lake,
Ascending heights of mountain peaks,
Climbing hillside pathways to the music of the streams,
The pictorial views and freedom bring such fun and joy.

Picnics with the sheep sitting in a great stone circle,
A sunset's colours fading,
Bring the tranquillity of night,
The peace of early morning heralds another day,
Incredible places to visit and friendships to grow.

Inspired By Love

As our week together is drawing to its close,
We sit around and ponder,
The precious memories we'll have,
We've learned from fantastic outings, seen amazing love,
A week of support this summertime has given us strength.

A Lakeland Dawn

The early morning,
Below the valley is obscured,
By a layer of cloud,
But above is a contrast of mood.

On one side,
Heavy grey clouds,
Cast sinister shadows onto rocky grey hills,
Yet within the same view,
Dappled sunlight kisses,
And trickles down grass-covered hillsides.

What will today bring?
No-one can tell,
But one thing is sure,
We cannot change it.

Inspired By Love

Our influence is powerless.
Wait!
The valley below begins to appear,
As the cloud creeps up the hillsides,
On both sides,
What will it reveal below?
Let's just wait and see!

A sunlit tarn,
A cloud-clad hill,
Two different stories,
In just one split scene.

A world revealed

A scene of unrivalled beauty,
Manicured by God not by man,
Gentle light kisses the hilltops,
While the valley below wakes gently,
Beneath a mist of calm serenity.

A lone bird rises higher and higher,
Using the natural thermals,
Reducing the need to exert energy or effort.

Inspired By Love

The mist slowly begins to rise,
As the sun climbs higher into the sky,
Revealing a land cleansed,
By night's peaceful tranquillity,
And the cool light of an orb-like moon,
Refreshed again after the blazing sun,
And scorching heat of the previous day.

Passing Through the Gates

Passing through the gates at Ashburnham,
You can feel the arms of love,
And peace envelop you,
As gently as a feather,
Might kiss you as it blows,
Weightlessly in the air.

Here is a haven of safety,
Untouched and unmarred,
By the outside world,
Filled with a heart of service,
Guided by the heart,
Of the one true servant.

Lord, yours is a heart longing to serve,
Bless and bring peace,
Into troubled hearts and lives.

Inspired By Love

This week help me to open my heart,
Allow you to heal,
And leave with the certain knowledge,
That you are always beside me,
Inside me, ahead of me and behind me.
Your presence forever to surround me,
And lift me up.

Ashburnham Blessing

Leaving a crazy, messed up world outside,
These gates lead to sanctuary.
A different air,
A different feeling,
A different atmosphere.
How special is this place,
A place of abundant blessing.
To know that special peace of God,
That passeth all understanding.
The world is at a distance,
The pressures and battles of life,
Can no longer imprison my aching heart,
As here in this haven,
I find true rest.
Equipping me to return once more,
But with an outlook renewed and refreshed.
Lord, help me not to lose sight of this
blessing,
And may I continue to know this rest.

Inspired By Love

Ashburnham Place

A place of light,
So filled with love,
Haven of peace and beauty,
Blessing people abundantly,
Uniting strangers through grace and mercy,
Reaching out across the world,
Newcomers welcomed with open arms,
Healing and hope,
Are both found here,
Ministering to every need, enveloped in the arms of God,
People not possessions are what are important,
Letting the glory of God shine out from under the dark cloud of
A fallen world, warmth lives at Ashburnham,
Creating a place of joy and serenity,
Exalting our Lord and Saviour.

Inspired By Love

Sanctuary

Enveloped by love,
Surrounded by peace,
A continuous circle of blessing,
Friendship and care,
Untainted and pure,
Joined together by God.
Ashburnham Place,
A haven for all,
Upheld by the arms of the Father.

Inspired By Love

<u>A Leaf</u>

I collected a leaf,
During a walk at Ashburnham,
This seemed to reflect my thoughts,
And feelings about this very special place.

The circular formation of leaves,
At the top,
Reflecting the complete,
And enveloping love,
And peace which I have found here,
On all my visits.

The two leaves below,
Representing the strong arms of God,
Continually holding and supporting,
All who live, work and simply pass through,
This special place of abundant blessing.

Inspired By Love

On The Way

On the way here I saw,
Out of the car window trees,
And bushes with such a variety of greens,
That were far too numerous to count.

They ranged from silver greens,
To dark blue-black greens,
Browny-orangey greens to yellow greens.

There were pale greens,
Reddish greens, dark greens, glowing greens,
Sparkling greens, quiet, calming greens,
Vibrant, joyful greens and many others in between.

These colours were constantly changing,
And blurring into each other,
Causing the pictures I saw,
To take on the likeness of a kaleidoscope,
Or mosaic of green jewels.

What a blessing on the journey here,
And to know even as the light changes,
So does every shade and hue.

Inspired By Love

Flight to far away

Above the clouds to unknown places,
Who knows what we'll find at the end,
Among a sea of unknown faces;
Above the clouds to unknown places,
Amid the chorus of different voices,
Searching for a familiar friend;
Above the clouds to unknown places,
Who knows what we'll find at the end.

Mystery destination

Where are we going?
Nobody knows,
A walk beside a rivulet flowing;
Where are we going?
No signposts are showing,
Fields all covered with winter's snows;
Where are we going?
Nobody Knows.

Inspired By Love

Ode to Losing My Way

Make a decision which way should I go?
Not on the main road, the countryside way,
It will take much longer we must go slow,
Where are we going on such a day?
To the left or the right? Straight on or go back?
Where we are now is a mystery to me,
We take the scenic route, not a wrong turn,
I love to explore but direction I lack,
Not really minding as long as I'm free,
Each bend I go round is a new road to learn.

I never get lost as I travel around,
It's just that my route is never well planned,
As long as my feet stay firm on the ground,
My journey will always be pleasant and grand,
New places to find, destinations unknown,
Taking a turn, not knowing where it leads,
Going over one bridge or under another,
Unhurried I travel, my time is my own,
Only constant photography my progress impedes,
Arriving back home I drink tea with my mother.

Inspired By Love

What I can see

I sit and look out at the world,
Through my window blows a gentle breeze,
And I can see across the fields,
What lies beyond the horizon?
My mind begins to imagine.

Where does that footpath lead?
What lies beyond the distant hill?
Something calls me back,
Back from my silent reverie,
A door slowly opens and I move my gaze.

As I peer through the door,
What greets my eyes?
The darkness of a corridor,
The distant light from another room,
Who just opened my door?

I hear it first before my eyes see it,
A small framed figure carrying a tray,
Who is she? What does she want?
She says nothing and then disappears,
I open my eyes, was it all a dream?

Inspired By Love

I sit and gaze out of the window,
A world reaching far beyond what I see,
What lies beyond the horizon?
Or behind that far distant hill?
Through my window blows a gentle breeze.

A Gossip's Observation

The view from the open door allows me a view,
Of a clock tower displaying the correct time.
Just beside this is a church spire.
A tree sits in front of the clock tower,
And leading to this are a variety of other buildings,
With vehicles parked outside them.

Coming back inside the café members of staff,
Wearing green t-shirts and black trousers,
Are busily serving customers,
Bringing food in and out of the kitchen,
Clearing tables and fulfilling the other duties,
Which their positions require of them.

Inspired By Love

As I sit, there are hushed conversations all around me,
A young couple with a baby in a pram have just entered,
She sat at a table,
But then her partner decided they should move.
A waitress calls out an order number,
Allowing her to locate the people whose order she needs to deliver.

An older couple sit in the corner by the window drinking coffee,
The gentleman is looking in my direction with a querying expression on his face,
Behind him are another couple,
The man appears much older than his female companion,
But both are wearing bright yellow t-shirts.
His is lemon and hers more sunflower coloured.

These four people have all just exited the café.
A lady in a red cardigan has just taken up position,
In the window which the elderly couple just left.

Inspired By Love

The Writing Room

Pictures of a time gone by,
Are hung on walls,
With embossed flowers that are creeping,
And climbing in all directions.

Looked down on by birds,
Of brass that stand statuesque,
On dark wood shelves.

A carpet of flowers at our feet,
Carrying through a botanical theme.

Sun glinting on brass ships,
Reflecting historical sea journeys,
Hand-painted decorative vases,
Bringing my mind back to flowers.

The piano in the corner,
Igniting pictures in my mind,
Of a parlour of an era long past.

Inspired By Love

What Lies Behind?

What can I see as I pass in the street?
The windows of many,
Behind each a new story.
One grabs my attention,
Ornate in design,
With shutters disguising what lies behind.
It is true there are flowers at the heart of this bay,
But why close the shutters?
Shutting out the day.
I stand and I ponder for many a minute,
Before I dare linger no more,
Moving along past the front door,
I notice another.
A pair to this window so shuttered and barred,
Maybe, just maybe this will tell me some more?
More of the mysteries that lie behind,
Such a large but shuttered clear door.

Inspired By Love

Shut In

I don't like this;
I can't see where I am going.
Is it dark outside?
Or just here,
In this box?

I never like going in here,
It usually means going somewhere I don't like,
But it is usually for less time than today.

Where am I going?
Reassuring voices keep trying to calm me,
Saying things like 'not long now',
And 'we'll be there soon'.

But right now this doesn't really help me.
What if I don't like this new place?
Then an idea begins,
To develop in my mind,
Maybe I can find my way,
Back to the old place.

Finally we stop moving,
Light floods in,
And I can smell outside air again.
Maybe this won't be so bad after all.

Natural World

Inspired By Love

Morning glory

Darkness fades as daylight dawns,
Bird song heralds every morn,
Life is stirring all around,
In the air and on the ground,
Flowers dancing at your feet,
Leaves that rustle, Wings that beat,
Dew on grass and spiders webs,
Tidal streams that flow and ebb,
Stop and listen, watch and see,
Nature in her morning glory.

Dawn

The dawn is breaking,
The horizon starts to glow,
Golden orb, flame red,
The sky alive and glowing,
The beauty of a sunrise.

Inspired By Love

Morning Message

As the mist moves away,
In the morn of the day,
Allowing the bright sunshine through,
I cannot but help,
Think of God and His love,
And Him being the Light of the world.

Surrounded

Into the valley from mountain above,
Comes water, flora and fauna given in love,
Mighty birds hanging on thermals up there,
Unseen yet so strong supported by air.
Leaves move above, at first just a whisper,
Before the sound all around me becomes even crisper.
Scents carry in from distances far,
Bringing aromas that thrill and ensnare,
The wind in the world,
The breath of our God.

Inspired By Love

Reflected in a thing of beauty

A spider weaves its web,
From the finest silken thread,
Each fragile strand carefully placed,
To form a delicate net.
Alone, each thread is easily broken,
But together they have strength.

These natural works of art,
Remind me of God's word,
That as Christians we are only part,
Of a united body,
And on our own,
In our own strength,
We are weak and vulnerable.
But when we work together,
Relying on the Lord,
Anything can be achieved,
Through Christ's amazing strength.

So together with God's family,
And with His power on our side,
We too can be a work of art,
And provide a web of love.

Inspired By Love

Serenity's gate

The gates stand open at the end of the lane,
Through leaf covered trees,
Sunlight dapples the ground,
The floral scent carried on the breeze,
The music of nature the only sound,
Unspoilt haven of peace and serenity,
Brings such tranquillity to those in need.

Who are you?

You are unseen,
But not invisible,
Your movement displayed,
In all that we view.

You are silent,
But you're never unheard.
Your power resounds,
In all that we hear.

Inspired By Love

You are untouched,
But can always be felt.
Your breath surrounds us,
In all that we do.

You have no scent,
But carry the perfumes,
You find as you move,
Through country and town.

You are tasteless,
But not without flavour,
You bring to our lips,
The salt from the sea.

You are unknown,
But not undiscovered.
Your name's familiar,
You are called The Wind.

Inspired By Love

<u>Caught in the Wind</u>

The lea of the rocks,
Little comfort offered,
Against what had started as a light playful breeze,
And was now more like a thundering tornado.

But the rocks were better
Than no protection at all.
Hunkering down lower and covering our heads,
With our cloaks we begin to hear a very different sound.

A sound much more terrifying than wind,
It was the roar of flames.
A fire here and now would be utterly devastating.
A wind of this magnitude and strength,
Will just blow it straight across a landscape,
Like this leaving no more than a charred wasteland.

Inspired By Love

Sounds of unfailing love

Water like liquid silver,
Flows gently over pebbles,
Turning them subtly,
Making melodies which are unrepeatable,
Using human or electronic methods.

A sound so pure,
That peace and hope,
Can both be found in this enchanting music.

The hope of a new beginning,
And the peace of a greater understanding,
Of just how much God loves us.
The knowledge that this water reflects,
The cleansing we have experienced,
Through Christ's sacrifice,
On our behalf is greatly comforting and reassuring.

Inspired By Love

Nature's melody

The music of nature fills the air,
With the gentle hum of contented bees,
As they visit each flower fair,
And the playful wind rustles through the trees;

Each little bird has its own sweet song,
And combined they give perfect harmony,
Early morn' there is such a throng,
They welcome each day with their symphony;

The grasshopper's rhythm plays its part,
The beat of the dragonflies' wings keeps time,
From each place they move like a dart,
Way off in the distance the church bells chime;

Stop and listen for a while each day,
Especially when you are feeling sad,
Watch and hear wildlife at play,
For nature's music will make you so glad.

Inspired By Love

The music of a waterfall

A fluid sound like liquid silver
Meets me through the trees,
Melting with a chime like rhythm
Floating on a silent breeze,
Round the bend my eyes catch sight of
This natural melody maker,
Threads of tiny sun-lit diamonds singing
As they fall to join a humming crystal stream,
Accompanied by a pebble percussion
Rolling, turning as the water flows,
A waterfalls majestic splendour
Playing out its own sweet song.

Inspired By Love

<u>Waterfalls</u>

Walls of water
Are
Thundering down,
Eager to meet the
River below
Foaming water shows where they unite,
And
Light from the sun
Like diamonds are
Sparkling.

Inspired By Love

Storm sonnet

Every eave creaks as wind howls round,
Piercing white light splits darkness asunder,
The rumble and crack herald the thunder,
No peace on a night like this can be found;
With torrents of rain that flood and destroy,
What will unfold in the cold light of dawn?
An ocean of brown instead of green lawn,
The old oak tree swept away like a toy;
Time passes unheard the storm still rages,
Our thoughts turn to fear for those out at sea,
Hoping for them that this storm lets them be;
I sit with a torch turning the pages,
Of a book well known throughout the ages,
Its comforting words help me to be free.

Inspired By Love

Clouds of Time

Pink tinged brush strokes,
Across an azure sky,
Slowly heralding the breaking dawn.
Gold creeps in with the rising sun,
A brand new day has truly begun.
Powder puffs float in an ocean of blue,
Joining and parting, bringing shadow and shade.
The sun starts to sink,
Gold trims each edge,
The sky turns from pink,
To flaming orange,
Then fiery red,
As the sun disappears, and evening falls,
The darkness of night encroaches,
And a lonely owl calls.

Inspired By Love

Contrasting clouds

Shade from the sun's heat,
Relief from its glare,
Or casting a shadow,
Of doubt and despair.

The promise of rain,
For the parched earth below,
Or dread of a deluge,
Bringing flooding and fear.

Clouds are a blessing,
And also a threat,
They can bring a healing,
As well as a hurt.

So look to the sky,
With wonder and awe,
And remember the rainbow,
God's promise to us all.

Inspired By Love

Clouds

Causing shadow,
Limiting light,
Outpouring moisture,
Uplifting drooping blooms,
Darkening the sky,
Sending sleep to a weary world.

Dawn Chorus

A bird
Sits on a branch
Singing so sweet and clear
Others join to help him welcome
The dawn.

Inspired By Love

Nature's Cacophony

Awake at early morn,
To see the breaking dawn,
A single bird begins to sing,
Heralding the hope,
Of one of nature's wonders,
A cacophony of sound.
Unrivalled in its beauty,
By any worldly music,
And a blessing to my ears.
Birdsong surrounds me,
Its harmonies lighten my heart,
The melody of the dawn chorus,
Amazing and profound.

Heralds of Hope

Sitting and watching,
Silent and still,
As birds come and visit,
To take their fill.

Inspired By Love

Blackbirds and bluetits,
Pigeons and wrens,
Bring life to a garden,
Lying dormant,
And gripped in winter's chill.

Hearing their song,
And seeing them feed,
Fulfils in me a longing and need,
Of the knowledge and hope,
That spring's on its way,
Getting closer and closer,
With each passing day.

<u>Birds</u>

Beating wings
In the air,
Reaching heights,
Displaying your colours,
Singing from dawn to dusk.

Inspired By Love

Kingfisher

King of the river bank
In looks and in speed,
Never to linger for long.
Gone in a
Flash.
Impressive to
See. Colours so vibrant,
Hunter supreme
Enters the water, appearing again
Reward held tight in your beak.

The kingfisher

Your feathers gleam,
Your colours flash,
You enter the stream,
With barely a splash,
Your vibrant blue appears again,
Your reward in your beak,
Is the first you'll attain,
I dare not speak,
For fear you'll take flight,
A fisher king,
Oh what a sight,
What joy a kingfisher can bring.

Inspired By Love

Kestrel

King on the wing, an
Excellent hunter
Silently hovering
To watch for your prey,
Ready to drop to
Earth like a dart,
Launching again, reward clear to see.

The Kestrel

A kestrel hovers on the wing,
Waiting on her prey to spring,
Silently watching all around,
Suddenly plummets to the ground,
With prey secured she'll rise again,
And fly to her nest,
To feed and to rest,
Before another hunting test.

Inspired By Love

Jay

Jewel coloured feathers with
A loud and rasping call,
You are one of nature's characters.

The Jay

The strangest call I ever heard,
Came from a very pretty bird,
A flash of blue, a flash of pink,
I really had my eyes to blink,
On the verge beneath the tree,
Sitting there looking straight at me,
It was a Jay,
And I must say,
I'd like to see it every day.

Inspired By Love

Barn owl 1

A flash of white in front of me,
Like a ghost it passed me by,
I stopped and watched as it caught its prey,
And then I saw it as clear as day,
It turned its head and looked at me,
It was a barn owl living free,
With a flap of its wings it rose once more,
And in the blackness of night did swoop and soar,
It lived in freedom that I'd never know.

Barn owl 2

The blackness of night surrounded her,
And nothing could be heard,
Then as she walked a ghostly flash,
Made her stop and watch,
Swooping down upon its prey,
A barn owl passed by as clear as day,
She wished she could live as freely as he,
As it flapped its wings to fly away,
Lost in the night once more.

Inspired By Love

Ode to an owl

Now with this feather may you be guided,
As daylight fades becoming night's darkness,
And as the sun sets this day has ended,
The moon in the sky with cool white brightness,
The barn owl from whom this feather did fall,
Will guide your path till you reach journey's end,
Friendship and welcome are sure to be found,
Only follow his call,
Watch for deceivers, the wrong way they'll send,
And soon you will reach the place whence you're bound.

Swans

Swans glide on a lake,
Every moment majestic,
Regal splendour shown.

Inspired By Love

Peacock

The eyes on his tail,
Display a regal glory,
The bright singing blue,
Iridescent gold and green,
The plumage of a peacock.

Flowers

Fragrant blooms and
Leaves
Of green,
Wild and living
Everywhere,
Resplendent in the
Sunlight.

Inspired By Love

<u>Bride of the Garden</u>

Pure and unspoilt,
The white lily stands,
Glowing in the sunlight,
Gently dancing in the breeze,
Spider-like tendrils enchantingly curl,
Framing the rest of this perfect bloom,
Untouched and resplendent,
Like a bride on her wedding day,
Coyly waiting for her groom to arrive,
This natural beauty perfectly reflected,
In the simplicity of a single white flower.

Inspired By Love

Break Open, Break Out

Protected,
Cocooned inside a velvet-lined shell,
But kept safe and secure by a strong, prickly armour.

Waiting,
Just waiting inside to open,
When this treasure is ripe and ready.

Then,
One day as it falls from the tree,
The armour begins to break open.

A sweet brown chestnut,
Revealed in a flower-shaped cradle,
At last it breaks out and is free.

Inspired By Love

Emerging

Rest is over,
Change complete,
No longer to crawl,
I now live to hover,
Hover on wings yet to unfurl,
But today I begin to live again,
Today I can really start anew.

First to break out,
Escape and fly free,
Dry my new wings,
That will lift me aloft,
Colourful flowers on which I can sit,
Are calling me now to visit,
Here I come, here I come, I'm free.

A caterpillar no more,
But a thing of such beauty,
To be admired,
My colours will glow,
I can truly be free,
Fly up to new heights,
At last I can be me,
I am who I am truly to be.

Inspired By Love

Breaking Out

Oh to be free like a butterfly,
To be able to fly where I please,
Not to be bound,
Or trapped, or enclosed,
Lord, help me break out and be me.

Oh just to soar like the eagle,
Over mountains and valleys below,
Not to be tethered,
Or caged, or captive,
Lord, help me break out and be me.

Oh to be free from my failures and fears,
To break out from the darkness that binds,
To trust with my heart,
To follow in faith,
Lord, help me break out and be me.

Inspired By Love

Soothing Sunsets

When turmoil and pressure surround me,
Closing in like the cloak of despair,
I escape to watch your glory,
Lighting up the sky.
A day of strife and trial,
Draws swiftly to a close,
But as I stand and watch your glory,
New peace settles in my heart,
The wonder of a sunset,
Across an empty field,
Your presence so very real,
The breeze is like a prayer.
The sun sinks ever lower,
The colours intensify,
Showing shadows,
Hearing echoes,
Of glories still to come,
Here in the closing minutes,
Of a hard and brutal day,
When all that is left is your love for me,
And even the silence cries,
In praise and adoration,
Of your glorious, holy name.

Inspired By Love

Contrasts

Light from the setting sun
Gently kissed the hilltops,
Speaking through the leaves
Was the light summer breeze.
As darkness fell the moon ruled the sky,
Gentle and calm was its silver light.
Below in the valley
Fiercely glowing like fire,
Electricity rules at the flick of a switch,
Bringing light to the darkened streets.
Above on the hilltop away from it all,
Lives are ruled by the wind.
Fireworks flashed, off in the distance,
A black velvet sky filled with hundreds of lights.
Chinese lanterns, carefully lit
Spiralling skyward, with fire and light.
Such peace and tranquillity up here cannot be bought,
By abiding unbreakable rules.
But fire and light
Rule inside our lives,
And reign supreme in our hearts.

Inspired By Love

Through the eyes of a child

Place of serenity high on a hill,
Where peace and beauty abound,
And time just appears to stand still;

A place where the sounds of nature resound,
Where life and pleasure are free,
And the grandeur is so profound;

A place where you stand and study a tree,
Where colour and movement meet,
And an unspoilt picture you see;

A place that when you look down at your feet,
Sweet purple heather grows wild,
And cool mountain air is a treat;

Take time to look through the eyes of a child,
Where innocence can be found,
And each memory may be mild.

Inspired By Love

<u>Gravity</u>

Gives us the ability to keep our feet on solid ground,
Rather than to float and drift suspended in mid-air,
A necessity for life on earth, but unseen, unheard, unscented, tasteless and untouched,
Valuable and witnessed only through its power.
In outer space its very presence is much less evident,
Though to say that its not there at all is certainly untrue.
Yes this is a quandary, baffling young and old, but its thanks to Mr Newton the world was ever told.

Inspired By Love

The Feather Floats

On each breath of wind,
The feather floats,
As though 'twas still attached,
To the wing of the bird,
From whence it came,
Though it has lost all direction now,
Unable to choose which way to go,
Or even where to land,
But its landing place is predetermined,
By the one whose guiding hand,
Guides the footsteps that I take,
Breathing on me courage,
Courage to go on.

Inspired By Love

Windows in the Ceiling

Above my head,
Set high in the roof,
Is where I can watch the clouds chase each other.

This window
Is one of two in this room
That cannot be reached,
Or viewed through from the ground.

It does not open in the usual way,
But can be opened using a long rod,
Hooked onto the bar and pulled down sharply.

Its position still allows
The sweet scents of spring
To drift in and down to me here.

I may not be able to see a scene through it,
But the clear blue sky,
Chasing clouds and birds in flight
Are enough for me right now.

Inspired By Love

A Hedgehogs Torment

Acorns are hitting me hard on the head,
Looking up I can see who's to blame,
Used as their missiles by naughty young squirrels,
Who delight in tormenting me year after year!
THUD! That was too close, another near miss,
Oh why can't they just let me be?
Up in the branches I can hear giggles,
And mean whispers all about me!
Mischievous merriment is what they would call it,
But I simply don't see the fun.
If you don't want to suffer a headache or worse,
Take some friendly advice from me,
Don't ever sit under an oak tree in autumn,
Any hedgehog I know will agree!

Inspired By Love

The bee

Where will I travel today?
As a bee I travel from flower to flower,
From one colour to another colour,
But not to enjoy the perfume,
Or even see the beauty,
No, I am to important,
To only stop and smell the roses,
I have my duty to perform.
I travel from one to another,
Each a new destination,
Collecting up the pollen,
With which I make some honey.
So when you hear me buzzing,
Or see me flying by,
Do not feel threatened,
If someday my honey you want to buy.

Family and Pets

Inspired By Love

My family - human and otherwise

My mother's name is Enid,
She likes to sing and act,
With you I'll only make one bid,
She'll only tell you fact;

My father's name is Alan,
A sporty minded soul,
Thinks of himself as a young man,
But can't now score a goal;

My brother's name is Andrew
He's into heavy rock,
He drinks an alcoholic brew,
And therefore needs a clock;

Now last of all I'm Helen,
The oldest child of two,
I often wish I had a den,
To escape to from Andrew;

Now my family's complete,
Apart from all our pets,
They all appreciate a treat,
But all dislike the vets.

Inspired By Love

A Silent Approach

An unlit night-black field,
Noiseless and still,
With a grass-covered path,
Leading to joy.
For someone who's life,
Was always fast-paced,
This was his haven of rest.
Walking to meet him as he returns,
From his latest fishing adventure,
No sign can we see,
No movement hear,
Until something flashes quite near,
Calling to him,
No answer comes back,
But this jumping light moves still nearer,
Until out of the inky black silence,
A voice shouts loudly, BOO!
His latest idea of a prank,
We jump clear off the ground,
His laughter ensues,
The light was attached to his wheel.
A simple bite detector,
On a single spoke,
Had held over us,
Such a power of fear.

Inspired By Love

Granddad

A great big man with a great big heart,
Full of love for whoever he met,
Always putting others ahead of himself,
If he couldn't help,
He would never do harm,
A life lived to serve,
And not to be served,
His death left a hole that could never be filled,
But summed up in words his epitaph reads,
A life of selfless service.

George

In May of 1905,
George Lionel Westwood was born,
As a child growing up in South Wales,
His journey to school was long,
Over the hills for five miles each day,
In weather from snow to hot sun,
As the oldest of all the children,
He often helped Dad on the farm,
At milk time each day,

Inspired By Love

Collecting the cows,
Riding Tommy the bull led the way,
As a young man he played football in goal,
But was dropped when his team lost by eleven,
He felt better however,
When later he found,
That the player who sealed his fate,
Went on to play for the national side,
So losing was not a disgrace,
When the mines ceased to be,
His brother and he moved to England to work for their uncle,
He began driving Lorries,
Long distance and short,
But things were not always much fun.
Then he met Agnes,
A young local girl who he soon grew to adore,
She liked him too and their feelings increased,
And in 1934 they were wed,
They soon had a son,
But nature was cruel,
And he died at just 10 days old,
George carried the coffin of his tiny boy,
And laid him to rest himself,
During the war he continued to drive,
Often transporting bombs,
His lorry got peppered with shrapnel,
Always willing to do his bit,

Inspired By Love

He was regularly out on fire watch,
During this time,
Three daughters arrived,
His bundles of joy they became,
And though things were tough,
He always made sure that his girls were never without,
As time went by each girl took her leave,
And was walked down the aisle on his arm,
But all of them knew without any doubt,
That their Dad would always be there,
George became older and retired from work,
But never sat idly by,
He looked for new ways in which to serve,
And served on the council for years,
When his age took this from him,
He didn't give up,
He sang in the choir at church,
The years crept along,
And his role became carer for Agnes,
With his great big hands,
He delicately sliced bread for her tea each day,
And never begrudged her a thing,
I have the honour to have known this man,
And to call him Granddad.

Inspired By Love

Poem for Dad

Time has flown since that day,
One year ago when we said goodbye,
Now all we have are memories,
To see us through when we are sad,
Your sufferings over,
For that I'm glad,
And though life goes on,
The pain remains.
We miss you so much,
That it's hard to say,
Goodbye to you again today.
We love you Dad,
And always will,
Knowing we'll see you again one day,
But for now,
We send our love,
With a gentle kiss,
On the wings of a dove,
Carried by the wind.

Inspired By Love

A Birthday Tribute

Dad,
Today we miss you even more,
As we remember this special date,
A day that should be full of joy,
Not sorrow, tears and heartache,
So we will do our best today,
To honour your memory,
With happiness and funny things,
With laughter and with love,
Happy Birthday Dad.

Inspired By Love

Andy

Andy you were special,
In so many ways,
Always full of mischief,
And fun throughout your days,
Never to be beaten,
Always with a smile.

On the day you left us,
And since you've journeyed on,
There's an aching in my heart,
Where my love for you goes on,
And so my dearest brother,
At rest now and at peace,
You will never be forgotten,
But you will be sadly missed.

Inspired By Love

<u>Two Years On</u>

Two years ago your light went out,
Taken too soon,
Taken too young,
From that day on hidden from our sight,
A special brother,
A loving son,
A cheeky torment,
But so much fun,
Still so missed,
Still so loved,
Andy,
To special to be forgotten,
You'll live in our hearts forever.

Inspired By Love

Time has gone

Andy,
Time has gone so very fast,
But you will never be known only in the past,
Three years ago you fell asleep,
But a place in my heart I'll always keep,
My love for you will never wain,
Until one day we meet again.
We miss you now and always will,
My baby brother I love you still,
Full of mischief and so much fun,
A dearest brother and loving son.

Treacle

Treacle was a cat,
Reliant on my care.
Energetic and full of life,
A lively, loving pet.
Crafty and cheeky,
Looking for mischief while at play and
Expertly hunting for mice.

Inspired By Love

Treacle

Treacle came to me at four months old,
She had been so frightened, lost and cold,
Her eyes full of longing,
Her face full of hope,
I just couldn't leave her,
She had to be mine;

We brought her home that very same day,
She found her basket and their she lay,
In front of the fire,
She slept all that night,
But played all next morning,
With vigour and fight;

As time went on she settled in well,
She leapt and jumped and never once fell,
So full of energy,
Always hungry too,
She wouldn't eat cat food,
Just chicken and fish;

Though she gets older she still has fun,
Spending her days in bed in the sun,
Playing with shoe laces,
Running up the stairs,
She belongs here always,
Forever with me.

Inspired By Love

Billy

Billy was a ferret,
Who we had from tiny babe,
Eyes tight shut and without any hair,
No bigger than my thumb,
Within just three short weeks,
His eyes were open wide,
And he was covered from head to foot,
In a polecat coloured fur coat,
It soon became apparent,
He was mischievous and full of fun,
And often being scolded,
By his ever patient mum,
At six weeks old his mum was stolen,
And Billy was bereft,
So to stop him getting lonely,
He often came indoors,
But one day he got under my feet,
And I stood on his poor little tail,
He jumped out of the way and ran round the room,
And the skunk like smell lingered for days,
As time went on he went on outings,
On a harness and a lead,
Not so keen on the outward journey,
But always ran back home,
On one of these excursions,
A treasure he did find,

Inspired By Love

Laying on the footpath a malteser caught his eye,
But his boy wouldn't let him eat it,
So he sulked and refused to move,
We took him to the hospital fete,
Where he enjoyed the children's fuss,
And his photograph was taken,
By a man from the local press,
When he attended the church bazaar,
The old ladies thought he was great,
But the vicar looked on from a distance,
Then turned and fled with fright,
After just a couple of years Billy became a dad,
And when two of his offspring went to live,
At the Sandringham royal estate,
He was filled so full of pride,
As the years went on he continued to be,
A favourite with us all,
And if he ever escaped from his cage,
He'd never run away,
He always headed straight for the house,
And waited at the back door,
His open friendly nature continued throughout his life,
And he liked nothing more than a cuddle,
And to fall fast asleep in my arms,
When he died at eight years old,
He left a Billy shaped void,

Inspired By Love

But we'll never forget his mischief,
And our memories won't fade.

Shadow Cat's Diary

My name is Shadow,
And this is where I,
Will tell you my tales,
Full of adventure and fun.
I love my food,
And I love to sleep,
And I love to make the birds disappear when
I creep.

My servant is ignoring me,
And working on her book,
So I thought I'd stop her in her tracks,
And sit upon her work.

I thought I'd been oh so clever,
I lost my tingling bell,
But now I'm just dismayed,
Because my servant bought a new one.
So now I'm back to the beginning,
She really is too mean,
I'll have to lose this other one,
Before I can appear unseen.

Inspired By Love

The weather today distressed me greatly,
I couldn't get out at all,
So I blamed my servants completely,
And put on my sternest face.

I am not a happy boy today,
My servants are so mean,
First they put my flea stuff on,
Disturbing my peaceful sleep,
And then they shut me in the kitchen,
So they could wake the noisy monster,
That cleans the carpet in my favourite room,
And now wonder why I will not love them.
They did give me all my food,
But really I do think,
That after such an awful day,
I deserve an extra treat.
But nothing is forthcoming,
So I will cry and mooch about,
Until they feel guilty,
Or I get bored and go to sleep.

I am so very proud today,
I caught myself a prize,
I took it home as a special gift,
But my slaves just put it outside.
I didn't want to eat it,
But catching it was fun,
I really couldn't understand,

Inspired By Love

Why they didn't want to keep it.
They did give me my dinner,
And now I've had tea too,
But if I catch another one,
I might not be so quick,
To share with them my hunting prowess,
I'll keep it to myself.

I have been away for days,
But now I am back home,
My family want me to behave,
But my opinion of them is grave,
I will forgive them fairly soon,
But first I'll make them suffer,
I'm being very vocal,
They won't forget my voice,
And I'm also being naughty,
Ha ha they have no choice.

Inspired By Love

I've been such a clever boy today,
So very proud am I,
Of my finely tuned in hunting skills,
Which I used to great effect.
The photo which you see below,
Shows how masterful I've been,
Although my servants didn't seem too pleased,
In fact they called me mean.
Three troublesome voles dispatched with ease,
It really was no hassle,
I didn't even have to chase about,
Just grab them as they fled.

Friendship and Feelings

Inspired By Love

The danger of doubt?

A doubting mind is flooded,
With unanswered questions and uncertainties,
Pertaining to their life,
Or even life in general.

Often living a life unfulfilled,
Hollow and empty,
Although they may not realise this.

Continually searching and seeking,
But never finding the truth,
Never being content,
Because regardless of their experiences,
And actions or activities,
Their lack of self-assurance or confidence,
Prevents them from truly believing in anything,
Or allowing themselves to accept their true worth.

Regrets are commonplace,
And joy is often rare or absent.
They very often cannot experience,
Peace of mind,
And never see themselves
As good enough or accepted.

Inspired By Love

These people have usually suffered,
From condemnation and a fear of failure,
Throughout their lives,
Often from people closest to them,
Who should have been able to promote,
And show love and encouragement.

These people do not need further condemnation,
But to know love and acceptance,
From us and be encouraged to find true peace of mind,
And security in God,
Who can heal all past hurts and fears.

We who know the truth,
Are responsible for guiding and supporting,
Those who don't,
Into a place where they can feel accepted,
And find hope.

We must pray for them daily,
And not reinforce the damage,
Which has already been done.
It is up to us to show them,
Another way to live,
And help them to find it!

Inspired By Love

This Too Shall Pass

Feelings are seasons,
Like times of the year,
Shaping and moulding our lives,
Some make us feel good,
Some make us think,
While others may make us feel sad.
But life is a journey,
To be travelled and lived,
Through battles and joys,
Through tempests and hopes,
And not to be suffered or feared.
God travels beside you,
Fulfilling each need,
If you just let him into your heart.
Feeling your pain,
Drying your tears,
Bringing you peace,
And showing you grace,
Blessing you throughout the years.
So take hold of His hand,
And open your heart,
To the joys He only can give,
Open your eyes,
That you may see,
The blessings poured out each day,
But most of all,
Use your ears to listen,

Inspired By Love

And hear your Saviour say,
'My child, all that you go through,
Whatever you may face,
Very soon,
This too shall pass.'

Passing Through the Feelings

A child brings such joy,
And a new found hope,
Completely dependant on you as they are,
But this unbridled joy,
May not be all you feel,
As a fear of what is to come creeps in,
Can I really provide all that he needs?
Am I really equipped to be,
A parent, a carer, companion and friend?
What if they don't like me?
You want to protect them from all suffering and pain,
But sometimes you just want to scream,
To return to a place,
Where you are the one,
Being comforted, cosseted, loved.
Time races on,
Nothings the same,

Inspired By Love

Even places where I could be me,
No longer exist the same as before.
But my child,
From the day you were born,
You became my son,
You turned my life upside down,
But whatever challenges each new day brings,
You are always precious to me.

Never Alone in my Darkness

When hope is lost,
And life is over,
For the ones we love so dear,
And we are broken hearted,
As we stand and shed a tear,
It's the knowledge you are with us,
Breathing hope into our hearts.
When the world is full of darkness,
No-one seems to hear,
The desperate call of those who are hurting,
Who suffer and who mourn.
But the King of Light is listening,
And knows each tortured soul,
He murmurs in the quiet,

Inspired By Love

He whispers in the dawn,
And at last these cords are broken,
Broken by His healing power,
A light is now appearing,
Lighting glory in the dark.
The people start to sing now,
Breathing hope in every heart,
And praise to you is ringing,
Bringing glory in the dark.

Shut Out

If only you would let us in,
We could help you.
But no,
You have built barriers around you for so long now;
No-one can even begin to get close.

I understand you are trying to protect yourself,
Prevent yourself from being hurt again,
But I'm not like that.
If only you would let me in,
I could show you how much you really are cared for,
How much you are loved.

Inspired By Love

Trust, I think is your biggest issue;
You have never really been able to trust
anyone have you?
Those people who were supposed to love you,
More than anyone else let you down,
You felt as though you had been abandoned
for a second time.

Now, as you face the final parting,
You shut us out even more.
We only want to be there for you,
To support you.

But we are now feeling some of the rejection,
You have felt throughout your life.
Some of the hurt that runs so deeply through
you,
Is now beginning to run through us.
We want to be there for you,
But while you continue to shut us out,
We can't be.

Perhaps when this season is over,
And you no longer feel you have to earn,
Their acceptance and approval,
Perhaps then you will be able to let us help
you.
Let us show you that there is another way to
live.

Inspired By Love

Finally, just maybe,
You will be able to accept and experience,
All that real love is.
It cannot be bought or earned,
It is a gift given freely from the heart,
To those who are closest to us.

Right now,
It is a gift I want to be able to give to you.
Please don't shut me out any longer.

Love lives on the wind

Grief is a hurt that won't subside,
A pain in your heart that you want to hide,
The people you miss,
On the wind, send a kiss,
And you know they have not left your side.

The love that you feel for each other still lives,
And as time goes by hurts will heal,
You will never forget loved ones who've
passed,
And memories last a lifetime.
The people you miss,
On the wind, send a kiss,
And you know they have not left your side.

Inspired By Love

<u>Love is in the clouds</u>

Above the clouds,
The sky is blue,
The sun shines bright,
With warmth and love,
This is a message from me to you,
I am always nearby,
Forever with you,
So do not be sad,
Or feel bereft,
I am at peace,
With my father above.

Inspired By Love

A loved one lost

When someone that you love has gone,
You feel grief and sorrow,
The tears you shed are not for them,
But for you who's left tomorrow,
You loved them dearly when they lived,
But now they've journeyed on,
It's difficult for you to see,
How that love can carry on;

People say their spirit still lives,
But this is little comfort,
You blame yourself for what occurred,
Though deep inside you know the truth,
You know for them that this was best,
But still an empty void exists,
Though time will help to ease the pain,
You will miss them evermore;

Though they have gone and you remain,
Your feelings will not alter,
You'll love them as you did before,
That heartfelt love can't die.

Inspired By Love

Commiserations

Don't give up or fade away,
This is not the end,
Although it's hard for you today,
Accept help from a friend.

Don't look back and miss the chance,
Have an aim and start,
Follow your heart and so enhance,
Your life in every part.

As days pass by you will find,
New things bring you hope,
You will look forward not behind,
And you will start to cope.

Who can tell what the future may hold,
But it is through disappointment we can learn
to be bold.

Inspired By Love

Laughter

Laughter is a tonic,
Amazing though it seems,
Unhappiness can be transformed,
Grins turn into beams,
Happiness spreads a message,
Telling those we meet,
Even when we feel sad,
Rejoicing makes us glad.

Inspired By Love

Silence

The silence of a snowfall,
On a winter's night,
Surrounded by the velvet pall,
Fills me with delight.
This enchanting winter wonderland,
Brings a tranquil peace,
Holding snowflakes in my hand,
Not wanting this moment to cease.
But the silence of an empty place,
Uninhabited and cold,
I feel my heart begin to race,
And don't want to cross the threshold.
This suffocating nothingness,
Fills me with utter dread,
Like walking through a wilderness,
With fear and panic in my head.
So my response to silence,
Depends on where I am,
And on circumstantial variance,
Not on who I am.

Inspired By Love

<u>Dreams</u>

Dreams can be both good and bad,
Some make you smile others sad,
Some just seem completely mad;

With a nightmare comes great fear,
Sometimes just a noise you hear,
Causes you to shed a tear;

Pleasant dreams can bring you hope,
Maybe even help you cope,
You'll no longer sit and mope;

So at night when you're asleep,
Pictures in your mind may creep,
Some will fade and some you'll keep.

Inspired By Love

Solitude - friend or foe

Time alone can sometimes be the time you need to think,
The gap you need to heal pain and come to terms with sorrow,
A period to contemplate and plan your life ahead,
But solitude can also be a time of fear and dread;

To be alone is sometimes the cause of misery,
A time which never can bring any comfort, joy or pleasure,
Loneliness can often mean the beginning of the end,
But it can mean a time to love and dream not one to regret;

Solitude provides a space which everybody needs,
The space we need to be ourselves and live independently,
We sometimes need to be alone to find the real us,
But loneliness can also be a greater fear than death;

Inspired By Love

For some to be alone can mean they are in danger,
They may be ill so that they hear and see things which are not real,
Harm may then come to them or others there would be no blame,
Though sometimes solitude can be the best and only cure;

Solitude can therefore be both friend and foe alike,
A happy time, a time of dread, a cure and danger also,
Time to think, time to fear, a time of sorrow or of joy,
Solitude can be all these but all souls need it sometimes.

Inspired By Love

Clouds of Despondency

Heavy grey clouds,
Hanging still and unmoving,
The atmosphere sinister,
With a darkness unyielding,
The misty moisture in the air,
Bringing dampness to a desolate scene.
The mood of this place,
As dark as the sky,
Isolation and loneliness,
Surrounding me,
Bringing fear and an anxious dread.
Uncertainty hovers,
I must escape,
But have lost my way,
And night's blackness is quickly stealing the day.

Inspired By Love

Windows of the Soul

What am I saying within my eyes?
Can people see what in my heart lies?
When I look at others do I really see?
What they are feeling, or is it just me?

Some eyes seem distant and far away,
As though their soul is trying to pray,
Others seem mournful as though in distress,
Can we get in and make their pain less?

Some eyes are darting, with terror are filled,
What can be said so this soul is stilled?
Others are calm and full of serenity,
What I wouldn't give to experience such purity.

Eyes can show love, laughter and grief,
Telling us surely how to live, but oh how brief,
Life can be cruel, life can be kind,
So our eyes are the windows to soul and mind.

Inspired By Love

I Stare Beyond

I stare beyond but do not see,
What lies outside is not for me,
The cobweb curtains mar the view,
I no longer see the sky so blue.

I sit in fear inside this house,
But take some comfort as I watch a mouse,
Scamper behind the tattered nets,
Only a glimmer of mottled light in gets.

My hope alone is as I sit here,
Shedding many a silent tear,
That all the cobwebs, dirt and grime,
Will block others from viewing my silent crime.

A knock at the door, oh no, not him,
My hope of remaining here grows dim,
The cobweb shrouds and remnants of net,
Behind windows of grime, I am vulnerable yet.

Inspired By Love

Memories

Can memories fade?
Or pain really heal with time,
History can't change,
But we must learn from the past,
And build a future that heals.

Reflection on Friday the thirteenth

Funny how dates
Remain
In our minds,
Dictating our daily
Activities.
Year after year
The feelings don't change,
Happiness and hurts,
Excitement and dread,
Things we remember shape
How lives are lived, memories
Imprint themselves in our heads.
Reflecting on the past,
Tackling the present,
Enriching each day or
Encroaching into our freedom,
Never allowing us to move on.
Today is just another day,
Happy or sad, the date is not to blame.

Inspired By Love

The Unexpected Letter

What was that?
The letterbox,
How strange,
The post already arrived.

Well, here I go,
To look at least;
Perhaps it's just the wind.

It sometimes playfully rattles the flap,
Particularly this time of the year.
No, it really is a letter,
Hand-delivered,
The writing unfamiliar,
Yet beautifully crafted.

I pick up the small white envelope,
Carefully between my finger and thumb.
No indication from whence it has come.
Perhaps it was meant for someone else.

Turning it over I begin to read,
The name and address.
No, not for someone else,
This is definitely meant for me.

Inspired By Love

I return to my seat at the table,
Trying to place the unusual,
Yet strangely familiar hand.
Something about it is telling me,
I should recognise it,
Know who it is from,
But I don't.

With anticipation,
And perhaps a little fear,
I begin to peel back the flap.

What is a secret?

Secrets
ar**e**
completely
reliant on
th**e**
trust of
other**s**

Inspired By Love

Friends

Friends are very special people, who are always there for you,
People who you can rely on to support you through and through,
Friends are people, who really care for you in times of trouble,
They share your joys, woes, hopes and fears and will not let you down;

Friends cheer you up when you are low they will provide a shoulder,
They will accept you as you are they won't want you to alter,
Friends stand beside you all through life they never will desert you,
It's thanks to friends that we can live a life so free from strife;

Without our friends our lives would be so lonely and so woeful,
A life alone for me would mean a world without tomorrow,
Friends are the people who in my mind make my life seem complete,
To make a friend just be yourself and most of all just smile;

Inspired By Love

It does not matter who friends are if they stay true and loyal,
Their race, religion, creed and colour make no difference to me,
The relationship between two friends should be everlasting,
All friendships have their ups and downs but should not ever cease.

<u>The touch of friendship</u>

The touch of a hand can bring comfort,
In a time of fear and distress,
Knowing someone is there with love and support,
And to offer a gentle caress.

This simple, pure act of such kindness,
Is certain to touch any heart,
The reassurance and healing from sadness,
And such sorrow is able to start.

True friendship will last when people part,
A bond which cannot be broken,
So though parting may pierce your soul like a dart,
A new precious gift has awoken.

Inspired By Love

This gift can be marked by a token,
Across a divide can transport,
A unity never to be forsaken,
A touch is a blessing of import.

Friends

Faithful and
Reliable, always there for you,
If
Ever they are
Needed,
Dependable and true.
So we must be there for them too.

Inspired By Love

Someone to confide in

A confident is someone who you can tell your troubles to,
Someone who is more than just an ordinary friend,
A person who is there to listen or maybe give advice,
But never hurt you or condemn,
Just support you through and through;

This special person need not be a relation or a friend,
It could just be a teacher, who has an ear to lend,
Or a shoulder to could be provided if the need arose,
They're there to be a help to you,
A comforter in sorrow;

A doctor, vicar or a neighbour could also fill this gap,
Or it could just be a friend, who has this special gift,
A friend you are especially close to and always can be found,
But most of all someone you trust,
And on whom you can rely;

Inspired By Love

Whoever this great person is it's up to us to use them,
When we need someone who's outside a situation,
It's difficult for us to tell a friend or a relation,
It's then we use our confident,
We know they can be neutral.

Thank you

Thank you for your gift, and
Help throughout the year,
Amazing friends like you
Need to
Know how much

You're loved,
Our friendship is a special one,
Unique to you and me.

Inspired By Love

This little note of thanks
Has come with gratitude
And love.
Not only for the gift you sent, but the
Kindness I've received.

You are such special people, who
Offer time and love, the
Unique gift of friendship comes from God above.

This little card comes from me to you, with
Heartfelt thanks
And gratitude.
Not only for the gift you sent, but also your
Kindness and friendship, now and the whole

Year through.
Our special friendship knows no bounds,
Uniting us in love each day in a special way.

Inspired By Love

United by the wind

As we part and I wave goodbye,
My heart is heavy but I will not cry,
The love we share in our hearts today,
Will bring you back to my arms I pray,
Wherever you are,
Be it near or far,
My love goes with you,
With words few but true,
So united we will be,
By the wind living free.

Celebrations

Inspired By Love

Love changes everything

The day has dawned,
The preparation is over,
The guests are seated,
The groom awaits,
The arrival of his bride,
On the arm of her father,
She appears at the door,
Dressed in fairytale gown,
Bouquet in hand,
Face delicately veiled,
And a train flowing gently behind her,
As she begins her journey down the aisle,
With tears in his eyes,
The groom sees his bride,
She smiles shyly unseen,
With love in their hearts,
Each one for the other,
From this moment on,
They are forever entwined,
Two have now become one.

Inspired By Love

Congratulations

A new baby boy,
A delight to behold,
A bundle of joy,
More precious than gold.
For husband and wife,
To cherish and care for,
This tiny new life,
They'll always adore.

And for their daughter,
Her own baby brother,
Love that won't alter,
Growing together.

So at this time may we say,
Congratulations on this special day.

Mother's day

Mother's day comes round each year,
And shouldn't be a day for fear,
A bottle of vodka is what he had,
A trip to hospital made mum sad,
But Andy learned a lesson that day and then
the air was clear.

Inspired By Love

A Mother's Special Love

The nature of a mother's love,
Is patient, unfailing and kind,
Her gentle spirit like a dove,
The most sincere that you could find.

From day one of your life she's there,
To hold you secure in her arms,
She wouldn't leave you anywhere,
When fear creeps in her voice just calms.

She'll pick you up when you fall down,
Your tearful eyes she'll gently dry,
She wants you to smile not to frown,
Her heart will ache each time you cry.

So once a year on Mother's Day,
We thank them for their love and care,
We show our thanks through what we say,
Rejoicing that our lives they share.

Inspired By Love

Birthdays

Birthdays are a celebration,
In respect of each year lived,
Regardless of how old we are,
They are days that we should cherish.
Have a party,
Dine with friends,
Appreciate the past and what lies ahead,
Years of life are precious,
So let's enjoy them while we can.

The carnival parade

It happens just one day a year,
The carnival parade is here,
At twelve-o-clock the entries gather,
There's bands and floats and us and other,
There's beauty queens galore;

Soon all the judging will take place,
It's then each group will find their ace,
There's two awards per category,
Now is the time you start to worry,
Is everything correct?

Inspired By Love

At last it's time results are due,
The ribbon on the cup is blue,
Hush! Our category's news is nigh,
The winner is bound to feel so high,
A thrill, a cheer we've won;

At two-o-clock it's time to go,
To give the crowded town a show,
The feeling of delight is intense,
The children smiling over each fence,
Today is full of fun;

We now approach the final street,
'Twill soon be time to rest our feet,
The parade is drawing to its close,
It ends beside where the river flows,
It's over till next year.

Inspired By Love

The London Olympics

Living a dream
Of Olympic gold
Nearing our journeys end.
Demanding events
Over days of competing
Not losing sight of our goal.
Olympian status
Long awaited reward after
Years of relentless training.
Medals of gold, silver and bronze
Personal bests and the crowds who
Inspire success.
Canoeing and sailing,
Gymnastics and swimming,
Athletics on track and on field.
Marathons, archery, shooting and diving,
Equestrian events and more.
Sporting legends and new stars combine in a
celebration of sporting achievement.

Faith, Hope and Love

Inspired By Love

Keep Your Eyes Open

Keep your eyes open,
Through daylight and darkness,
Wonder's can always be found,
From cotton wool clouds in an ocean of blue,
To pin pricks of stars in the black velvet night,
A flower in a meadow,
Fruit on a tree,
Keep looking around you,
For the Blessings you'll see.

Keep your eyes open,
Through triumphs and trials,
Comfort can always be found,
From the words of a brother or sister in Christ,
To the actions of a stranger unknown,
The joy found in birdsong,
The touch of a hand,
Keep looking around you,
For the Blessings He brings.

Inspired By Love

Father, I thank you,
For all that you do,
In the past, every day and to come,
My secureness, my strength,
My rock and my light,
Never once letting go of my hand,
I'll keep looking around me,
But never behind,
For the Blessings I have in you.

Inspired By Love

Break Out, Be Free

When darkness looms,
And trials come,
Look to the Lord,
Break out,
Be free.

When your heart aches,
And pain resides,
Cry to the Lord,
Break out,
Be free.

When fear sets in,
And locks the door,
Trust in the Lord,
Break out,
Be free.

When freedom comes,
And light floods in,
Live in the truth,
Break out,
Be free.

Inspired By Love

God Has Made A Promise

God has made a promise,
To keep you safe in His arms,
To break the chains that bind you,
So you can be truly free.

God has made a promise,
He will never let you down,
He will dry your tear-stained eyes,
So you can be truly free.

God has made a promise,
In Him you will not stumble,
He will raise you when you fall,
So you can be truly free.

God has made a promise,
To support you when you're weak,
You will find true strength in Him,
So you can be truly free.

God has made a promise,
To bind up each broken heart,
To put an end to sorrow,
So you can be truly free.

Inspired By Love

God wants us to promise,
To love Him with our whole heart,
And to serve Him to the end,
To lift His name with singing,
And to live a life of prayer,
To take each step with faith,
And to honour the one true God,
Then we can be truly free.

<u>Blessing and Breakthrough</u>

Thank you Lord for a week of such Blessing,
A week truly rooted in You,
Surrounded by Love,
Upheld by Your Grace,
And by the Power,
Of Your Holy Spirit,
A week filled with real breakthrough.

Inspired By Love

Lord, I Find You

In my darkest pit Lord,
I find you,
Help me to never let go.

When my heart breaks with sorrow,
I find you,
Help me to never let go.

When I cry with my tears of such sadness,
I find you,
Help me to never let go.

Amidst a cloak of suffering and grief Lord,
I find you,
Help me to never let go.

Wherever I am Lord,
I find you,
Thank you for loving me so.

Inspired By Love

We are greatly loved

To enter a garden where we are dwarfed,
By the flowers,
Brings into sharp focus,
How insignificant we as humans,
Can sometimes see ourselves.

We often feel worthless or lost,
In a world of expectations,
That we cannot fulfil,
Especially when facing uncomfortable,
Or unwanted challenges in our lives.

It is at these times however,
The Lord can really work through us and in us,
If we trust him,
And allow him to lead the way,
Down paths which He is directing for us.

We are never insignificant in God's eyes,
And are so valuable and precious to Him,
That He sent His only Son,
To pay the ultimate sacrifice,
So that we may know how truly loved and cherished we are.

Inspired By Love

The Wonder of Wind

The wind in my face,
Stings my eyes, slows my pace,
The wind at my back,
Urges me on, keeps me on track.

The cold wind of winter,
Numbs me, chills me, is bitter,
The warm wind of summer,
Calms me refreshes me is comfort.

The breath of the Lord,
Is healing and gentle,
Not harsh and unloving,
But healing and fragrant.

Allow me to see the wind on my face,
As God breathing His Spirit o'er me,
Help me to know the breadth of his love,
Is my strength when I stumble and fall.

Inspired By Love

Unlock My Mind

Unlock my mind,
So I can know,
The freedom enjoyed by the wind.

Unlock my heart,
So I can feel,
The freedom enjoyed by the wind.

Unlock my tongue,
So I can tell,
Of the freedom enjoyed by the wind.

Unlock my Spirit,
So I may soar,
As an eagle rides, carried by the wind.

Oh breathe of God,
Unlock my life,
So I can live,
In true freedom like the wind.

God's Grace

Oh breath of God come breathe on me,
Fill me once again,
Come calm my spirit,
Grant me your sacred peace.

Allow me to rest in your arms Lord,
Quieten my mind,
Open my soul to your healing touch,
Grant me your sacred peace.

Inspired By Love

Power and Peace

The wind is busy, gathering, blowing,
Clouds are converging, colliding, amassing,
My mind is reflecting, swirling, darkening,
With the wind comes the weather,
With my mood comes the heartache.

Now comes the rain, falling, stinging, battering,
Nature runs for cover, scurrying, burrowing, hiding,
My tears are falling, hot, salty, unceasing,
The storm is great, powerful, unyielding,
My mood is deep, lowering, oppressive.

The clouds are breaking, clearing, fading,
The wind is lessening, working, calming,
My mind is numb, waiting, searching,
The wind can bring both good and bad,
The breath of God is healing restoring, blessing.

Thank you for the power of the wind,
Thank you for the touch of you love,
The strength of the wind,
The gentle breath of God,
Are these not just one and the same?
Amazing God, Amazing Grace.

Inspired By Love

<u>Webs of words</u>

Woven in the Father's image,
Enfolded in His love,
But trusted with a mission, to
Share and spread His word.

Overcoming fear and failure,
Faith in Jesus helps us through.

Witnessing for our Redeemer,
Opening our arms in love,
Reaching out to those who are hurting,
Deepening our faith and knowledge,
Shining light into our world.

Inspired By Love

The power of words

Weaving words together,
Forming poetry and prose,
Bringing joy to other's hearts,
And light to a darkened world.
I like to use my writing,
To spread the love of God,
And share Christ's gospel message,
With the lonely, hurt and lost.
We are called to use our talents,
In the work we do each day,
And this gives me so much pleasure,
I like to share it night and day.

Inspired By Love

The Labyrinth of Life

Life is like a journey,
To discover and explore,
Not always how we plan it,
Sometimes causing pain,
Joy and laughter too can be,
As we travel through,
But we don't have to travel alone,
Or get lost within a maze,
Jesus has a plan for us,
And he will lead the way,
If we choose to follow him,
And not to go astray,
We will find him at the centre,
Of our labyrinth each day.

Inspired By Love

<u>The constant companion</u>

Who will be there when I feel alone?
Who'll give me strength when I feel weak?
Who'll give me courage when I am afraid?
My Jesus, My Saviour, My Friend;

Who can I tell when there's no-one to listen,
Who can I ask when I don't know the answer?
Who'll give me comfort when I shed a tear?
My Jesus, My Saviour, My Friend;

You'll never forsake me or leave me abandoned,
You won't turn away and forget that I'm here,
Wherever I go you'll always be with me,
Thank you My Jesus, My Saviour, My Friend.

Inspired By Love

The Message

I am forever among you,
Wherever you maybe,
My people are my passion,
Keep your eyes on me.

I will always walk beside you,
Whatever you may face,
My children you are special,
In me you can be free.

I will always listen to you,
I hear each heart-felt prayer,
You are a royal priesthood,
I chose you for who you are.

So my blessing rests upon you,
Each and everyone,
Give yourselves into my care,
So my plans for you may flourish.

Inspired By Love

Never alone

In the darkest night,
You shine your light,
In the depths of despair,
You are always there,
When I'm full of fear,
I know you are near,
When I sit and cry,
My eyes you dry,
No matter what I face each day,
Lord, you remain faithful all the way.

Inspired By Love

My Precious Child

My precious child,
You are never alone,
Whatever you go through,
I am walking beside you,
You are mine and I love you,
I will not let you go,
Hold my hand,
Do not be afraid,
You will not stumble,
You will not fall,
You are safe with me,
My arms of love surround you,
Just call on my name,
I will answer you,
Let me carry your burdens,
Trust me with everything,
Trust me forever.

Inspired By Love

<u>Let me comfort thee</u>

In this place of serene tranquillity,
Watching sunlit diamonds glint on the sea,
Hearing God whisper His peace through the trees,
My dear sweet child let me comfort thee.

The hum of the bees lazily buzzing,
The warmth of the fireball sun on my back,
Feeling His presence envelop my heart,
My dear sweet child let me comfort thee.

The silence of butterflies dancing on air,
White wisps of the gentlest dove high up in an ocean of blue,
Seeing His love in all that surrounds me,
My dear sweet child let me comfort thee.

Inspired By Love

<u>My Dove of Light</u>

A shaft of intense morning sunlight,
Caught in the corner of a tiled room,
A dove of light appears before my eyes,
I needed so much this feeling of peace,
This message from the Lord,
John, Chapter fourteen verse twenty-seven,
'Peace I leave with you;
My peace I give you.
I do not give to you as the world gives.
Do not let your hearts be troubled and do not be afraid.'
Thank you Lord,
You are constant and consistent,
My ever present help and guide,
Keep me walking close to you,
Do not let me wander,
Help me recognise your blessings,
And keep my focus straight and true,
Always looking Saviour, to you.

Inspired By Love

Light of the World

Candles give light on a metal globe,
Each one lit for a different reason,
Some for hope and some for healing,
Some for peace and some in pleading,
Some in love and some in forgiveness,
Some to say thank you for our lord Jesus,
But all are lit to remind your people,
That you are the only true light in this world.

God is our Light

Darkness is deceitful,
With light comes hope and help.
Through our gracious Lord's great mercy,
We can know the truth, and freedom
That comes through faith in Him.
To trust Him is to live in light,
And know His awesome power,
But also such a peace and love,
That in darkness holds us still.

Inspired By Love

Heaven's reflection

Mist in a valley,
Cloud topped hills,
Golden light streams between,
Like shards reflecting heaven,
The streets paved with gold,
The glory of God,
Surrounding me.

God's awesome greatness

As I stand looking out,
Towards the far horizon,
Where the sea meets the sky,
It is then I see your awesome power,
Your work in all it's majesty;

The sun is shining from behind me,
Glinting like diamonds on the sea,
The air is cool and crisp,
This scene speaks of your love to me,
Your light within my darkness;

Inspired By Love

The gentle waves lapping on the sand,
The breeze rustling the leaves on the trees,
The sounds of your creation all around,
Through this your greatness is displayed,
Your rivers of mercy continually flow.

Everlasting love

A rainbow is a promise,
Sent from our God above,
A sign to bring a Christian hope,
To tell of His great love.

A love that's everlasting,
And given by a friend,
A friend who never leaves your side,
And wants your heart to mend.

Thank you O my God and king,
You're faithful to the end,
You keep me safe in your embrace,
Your Spirit you will send.

Inspired By Love

Creative

Created in the Father's image,
Redeemed by His great love,
Eternal life we gain through Him,
Amazing grace we receive from Him,
Trust in Him with all your heart,
In Him the weak are strong,
Victory is ours with Him,
Everlasting God.

Chosen

You are special,
I chose you!
I love you, for who you are,
You don't need to try to be what you're not.
My plan for you is tailor-made,
And you fit it perfectly.

Inspired By Love

Chosen by God

Lord, as I look out on your creation,
I cannot take it in,
Why somebody so small and wretched,
Was chosen by the King,
Your love for me is infinite,
Your mercy overflows,
Your grace increases by the day,
As I struggle Lord to pray,
Everything you make is perfect,
Father may my praise to you ring out forever.

Inspired By Love

Come to me

Come to me my child,
And rest in my arms of love,
Talk to me my child,
And receive from me my peace,
Listen to me my child,
And you will be given hope,
Walk with me my child,
And I will show you the way,
Bring all your cares,
Bring all your burdens,
Lay all at the foot of the cross,
Trust me to look after them,
And receive my strength everyday.

Inspired By Love

A test of faith

When everywhere I look is dark,
Keep my eyes on your sovereign light,
When life's storms are all about,
Keep my feet secure on the rock,
Lord when all around me seems utterly hopeless,
Help me trust in you;
No matter how bleak the path I tread,
Keep me clinging to your eternal hope,
Whenever I feel completely alone,
Keep me safe in your righteous love,
When everything presses in and encloses me,
Help me know true freedom in you.

An ever present help

If you follow,
He will lead the way,
Helping you face the trials of each day;

If you trust,
He will stay by your side,
If only you let Him be your guide;

If you believe,
He will never leave you,
But continues to love with a heart ever true.

Inspired By Love

<u>Amazing Love</u>

On my own yet not alone,
Surrounded by your love.
When I cry you dry my eyes,
When I fall you help me rise.
When I am weak you make me strong,
And find me when I'm lost.

Lord, you love me in my imperfection.
Your grace and mercy know no bounds.
Help me trust you in my frailty,
To walk in the knowledge I'm secure in you.
Father you are awesome,
I thank you God for who you are,
And who you want me to be.

Inspired By Love

A journey of faith

Every step you take in faith,
The Lord will guide your path,
Throughout the trials of each day,
He will be with you all the way,
His grace is overwhelming;

Trust in Him with all your heart,
The Lord will never let you down,
Although we go through testing times,
He will be forever near,
His mercy is abounding.

Comfort through faith

When I don't know which way to turn,
I look towards my God and pray,
The tribulations life throws at me,
Are never as hard with Him at my side,
Always giving me courage to cope,
And forever giving me reason to hope,
The guidance I'm given day by day,
Comes from Christ Jesus,
The light of the world.

Inspired By Love

Always there

As I travel along life's highway,
I know the Lord is by my side,
Meeting the challenge of each new day;
As I travel along life's highway,
I hear the voice of Jesus say,
Let me be your guide;
As I travel along life's highway,
I know the Lord is by my side.

A touch from God

The touch of a feather,
The touch of the wind,
The touch of your grace on my life.

The touch of affection,
The touch of acceptance,
The touch of your merciful love.

The touch of such power,
The touch of such care,
The touch that reaches me everywhere.

Inspired By Love

The touch of your Spirit,
The touch of your Son,
The touch of my Saviour and Father above.

Your touch on my life,
Your most precious gift,
Given selflessly and freely to me.

A reassuring presence

I am never alone with you at my side,
Your Spirit is always there as my guide,
To trust in you gives me peace of mind,
My Jesus you are so loving and kind.

Redeemer

Reliable in
Every way, you are my
Dearest friend.
Encouraging me
Every day in your
Most loving way.
Expecting only this from me, to
Respond to others in love.

Inspired By Love

Reassurance with God

Your word is a lamp to light my way,
Your love surrounds me throughout the day,
Your Spirit is always there to guide me,
It is by your mercy that I am free.

Christ's example

Christ's passion is for those in need,
The orphan and the widow,
A Father for the fatherless,
Companion for the lonely,
A Comforter for those who mourn,
A Healer for the sick,
His heart is one of mercy,
His grace is there for all.
So as Christians it's our duty,
To follow in His path,
To live by His example,
In all we do and say,
With each new day that comes along,
There's another chance to serve,
And live our lives as Jesus leads,
So we don't go astray.

Inspired By Love

Holy Spirit

Help us to listen
Only to you,
Learning to live as
You want us to.
Serving each other,
Providing comfort and care.
In all we do, may we
Reflect you.
In all that we say, may
These words show your love.

A prayer poem

You will not let me stumble,
You will not let me fall,
You want me to be humble,
And to hear your call,
O Lord help me to hear,
And please stay forever near,
I want to praise you always,
Throughout all of my days.

Inspired By Love

A guiding light

As I travel along life's path,
The word of the Lord lights my way,
If I go astray for forgiveness I pray,
And his grace brings me back,
To the way I should go,
If I grow weary and can't journey on,
It is then that my Saviour will carry me;
When I don't know which way to turn,
I look towards my God and pray,
The tribulations life throws at me,
Are never as hard with Him at my side,
Always giving me courage to cope,
And forever giving me reason to hope,
The guidance I'm given day by day,
Comes from Christ Jesus,
The light of the world.

What do we hold in our hearts?

When we are young,
Life is such fun,
With songs we have sung,
And the tales we have spun,
What joy we can hold in our hearts.

Inspired By Love

As we grow up,
Life is like rain,
Our time like our cup,
Full, yet empty again,
What burdens we hold in our hearts.

Once we are old,
Our life slows down,
Time precious like gold,
Trying to smile not to frown,
What fear we now hold in our hearts.

What does age mean?
How do we change?
Does time just pass by?
Oh, why are we so strange?
What is it we hold in our hearts?

Life must be lived,
Young, old, between,
In God you are loved,
Valued, and not unseen,
We need to hold God in our hearts.

Inspired By Love

God's anchor

Anchored by His love,
Precious love sent from above,
Gentle as a dove.

The Value of Time

I haven't got time,
There is so much to do,
Clearing the clutter and the grime,
All I want is to see my way through.

Take a break,
You have got to be joking,
I cannot sit beside a lake,
When demands of the world leave me choking.

How can I possibly ever be still?
When society demands we move at a pace,
What can I find to give me that thrill?
Stop my child, look into my face.

Inspired By Love

Lord, is that you?
Are you talking to me?
Lay down your burdens and follow me do,
Open your heart I will help you to see.

The ways of this world are not so important,
Your heart and obedience are all that I ask for,
Rest in me child, you will be triumphant.
Thank you my father, like the eagle I'll soar.

Christ

Compassionate
Hearts are what He
Requires.
In His name we are told to
Serve. Sharing
The love of God.

Inspired By Love

Saviour

Servant
And
Victorious
Is
Our
Unique
Redeemer

Pentecost

Pray
Earnestly
Now
To
Experience
Christ
Our
Saviour
Today

Inspired By Love

Strength

Support
Truth
Repel
Evil
Nurture
Grace
Trust
Him

Weary

When you need
Encouragement remember
Almighty God
Rejoices in
You

Inspired By Love

Power

Prayer
Out of
Weakness
Encourages people
Regularly

Weak

We learn through
Experience
And then gain
Knowledge

Tired

Trust
In God to be
Renewed
Every
Day

Inspired By Love

Stumble

Stronger
Together
United
May we
Bless and
Love
Everyone

Fall

Father
Above
Light of our
Lives

Inspired By Love

Hope

Helping
Other
People
Everyday

Lord

Love
Outpoured
Revealing
Delight

Renew

Rejoice in the Lord
Every day and
New
Energy to keep going
Will fill you

Inspired By Love

Soar

Serve
Others
And be
Rewarded

Wings

Wisdom
Is knowing our
Need of
God's
Strength

Eagles

Everlasting
Almighty
God
Loves
Everyone
Selflessly

Inspired By Love

Run

Repentance
Unites
Nations

Walk

Walk
Always
Loving the
King

Faint

Father
Above
In your
Name we
Trust

Inspired By Love

When times are tough

When times are tough,
I lose my way,
Your gentle touch will bring me back,
And I can start again.

Through your eternal peace,
That surrounds me everyday,
My ability to cope, oh Lord,
Is granted by your power.

When I go deaf,
Or do not see,
Your endless grace will bring me back,
And I can start again.

When life is good,
And I forget,
Your mercy Lord will bring me back,
And I can start again.

Through all my days,
Lord, help me know,
You light each step and are my guide,
Lord, help me start again.

Inspired By Love

Whenever I call

Whenever I call on your name,
You hear me,
Whenever I cry out in pain,
You hear me,
Lord, you show so much love to me.

Whenever I'm shedding a tear,
You're with me,
Whenever I'm scared and alone,
You're with me,
Lord, you are so gentle with me.

Whenever I stumble and fall,
You hold me,
Whenever I can't carry on,
You hold me,
Lord, you provide such strength for me.

Whenever I can't find my way,
You guide me,
Whenever I struggle to pray,
You guide me,
Lord you are always there for me.

Inspired By Love

Travelling with God

Travelling along the pathway of life,
Unsure which way I should go,
If I follow my own way it's sure to go wrong,
So I look to my God and pray.

I ask for His help,
He will make my way clear,
I ask for His help,
And I won't need to fear.

Travelling along the pathway of life,
Afraid to take the next step,
If I push a door will I get the right answer?
So I call on my God and pray.

Travelling along the pathway of life,
Following God all the way,
Rejoicing and trusting in God's plan for my life,
So as I follow my God, I pray.

I asked for His help,
And He made my way clear,
I asked for His help,
And my fears disappeared.

Inspired By Love

So I say thank you my God,
O thank you my God,
Thank you my God forever.

<u>Listen, listen a voice is calling</u>

Through the wilderness,
Make a straight path,
A highway for our God;

Listen, listen, a voice is calling,
In the desert prepare a way,
Listen, listen, a voice is calling,
Prepare a way for the Lord.

Raise the valleys up,
Level rough ground,
The mountains are brought low;

Listen, listen, a voice is calling,
In the desert prepare a way,
Listen, listen, a voice is calling,
Prepare a way for the Lord.

Inspired By Love

Lord your glory shines,
The world will see,
For Jesus has declared;

Listen, listen, a voice is calling,
In the desert prepare a way,
Listen, listen, a voice is calling,
Prepare a way for the Lord.

Safe in your arms of love

You come to me in my darkness,
You lift me out of the pit,
You shed a light on my path,
You give me a reason to hope;

Your grace overwhelms me,
Your mercy abounds,
I am safe in your arms of love;

You speak to me in my distress,
You wipe the tears from my eyes,
You keep me safe on the rock,
Your strength in my life helps me cope;

Your grace overwhelms me,
Your mercy abounds,
I am safe in your arms of love;

Inspired By Love

You always show me your kindness,
You are always by my side,
You show forgiveness each day,
You give me the courage I need;

Your grace overwhelms me,
Your mercy abounds,
I am safe in your arms of love;

God's faithful love

Do not give up,
Do not lose hope,
The Lord is there,
He will help you cope.

He gives you strength,
He comes to save,
Courage He'll give,
He will make you brave.

When tears are shed,
Your eyes He'll dry,
Held in His arms,
It is safe to cry.

Inspired By Love

Special you are,
Cared for with love,
Christ is with you,
Gentle like a dove.

Our debt can never be re-paid

May we never cease to worship Jesus,
May we always sing His praise?
Keep our eyes focused on the cross,
Never to forget the cost,
The sacrifice He made for us.

Thank you Saviour,
Thank you Lord,
Our debt can never be re-paid.

Help us always to trust in your word Lord,
Help us not to lose our way,
In everything we do and say,
Let your love be on display,
So you are always in control.

Thank you Saviour,
Thank you Lord,
Our debt can never be re-paid.

Inspired By Love

Keep me close

With joy let us praise Him,
With gladness we worship,
He lives in our hearts,
And we live in Him,
We're acknowledging Christ every day.

You are my Rock,
My Redeemer,
My Saviour,
My Friend,
Lord keep me close to you always.

O we are His people,
The sheep of His pasture,
We go through His gates,
And enter His courts,
With our songs of thanksgiving and praise.

You are my Rock,
My Redeemer,
My Saviour,
My Friend,
Lord keep me close to you always.

Inspired By Love

Give thanks to the Father,
Sing praise for His glory,
The Lord is so good,
His love never fails,
God is faithful and loving always.

You are my Rock,
My Redeemer,
My Saviour,
My Friend,
Lord keep me close to you always.

God of Hope

Trust in the God of hope,
His joy will flood your soul,
His peace will fill your heart,
And by His Spirit's power,
You will overflow with hope.

War and Conflict

Inspired By Love

The Futility of War

One hundred years ago,
In the year 1914,
Our young men went off to fight,
A war that we were told,
Was a war to end all wars,
This pointless waste of life,
And the innocent who suffered,
Just simply wasn't right.

Blood was shed,
Lives were lost,
The stench of death hung in the air,
So many paid the ultimate cost,
Needless and for nothing.

Sorrow lingered all around,
Mourning was the only sound,
A single hollow bell rang out.

Even for those whose loved ones returned,
Lives were forever changed,
Their hearts seemed buried too,
In the corner of a foreign field,
Beside their comrades fallen,
Beneath the waving poppy heads,
Never again to be woken.

Inspired By Love

Evacuation-
A child's perspective

Sent to where I was a stranger,
Alone and without those I love,
To keep me away from the bombs constant danger.

I sat by the window, a passenger,
Watching birds in the sky far above,
Sent to where I was a stranger.

Every day made to feel like a scrounger,
Wanting to hide like the bee in a foxglove,
To keep me away from the bombs constant danger.
Praying each day for a messenger,
To escape on wings like a dove,
Sent to where I was a stranger.

Placed here by an unknown arranger,
Pushed through the door with a shove,
To keep me away from the bombs constant danger.

Inspired By Love

Seen by their child as a challenger,
Unaccepted, without any love,
Sent to where I was a stranger,
To keep me away from the bombs constant danger.

Separation sorrow

I was 10 years old when war broke out,
Too young to fully understand,
I knew that dad was flying a plane,
And mum was frightened all the time,
I tried to make her feel better,
And she tried not to let it show,
But her face gave her feelings away,
As I turned to say goodbye,
My eyes caught a glimpse of mum's tear-pricked red eyes,
Why was I being sent away?
To keep me safe had been mum's reply,
Shouldn't I be staying with her?
To help her till dad came back home,
The terror I felt could not be explained,
But grew and grew inside me all day,
The journey began,
Tears started to flow,

Inspired By Love

The city of London was all I'd ever known,
As the train took me further and further from home,
The view from the window continued to change,
Trees replaced buildings,
Roads became fields,
The sun of the morning had faded away,
The sky had changed colour,
And instead of soft blue,
Now looked more like grey marble,
As clouds gathered and grew,
Feeling abandoned, I looked at my luggage,
My small battered suitcase and brown paper bag,
With food inside I was told not to touch,
Some tins had meat in,
Others had fruit,
And two packets of biscuits as gifts for strangers,
My gas mask hung in a box round my neck,
On my coat hung a label on which was my name,
My mind flew back to leaving mum,
I had tried to be brave and not to cry,
In her embrace I had felt so secure,
I had longed for her arms to hold me forever,
But from that moment on,
I was all on my own.

Inspired By Love

__Only wanted for the money__

The journey behind us,
We walked down a road,
But not like the ones I'd always known,
With little white fences,
And horses and carts,
It was different to London and all of its cars,
The buildings looked strange with their roofs made of straw,
And many had gardens with flowers in bloom,
I'd never seen houses like this before,
After a while my legs started to ache,
I was glad when we stopped at a church,
To its side was a hall that was all in shadow,
It was gloomy and dark and friendless inside,
With my back against the wall,
I stood like the rest,
We'd been told we'd be chosen by someone who came,
But as strangers left taking some of my friends,
I knew that I wouldn't be wanted,
At last a couple with a child of their own,
Came and agreed to take me home,
As I left the hall I heard the man say,
`Well at least by taking her we'll get paid`,
My mouth felt dry,

Inspired By Love

And my stomach felt tight,
I knew that I wouldn't sleep much that night,
Their little girl didn't murmur a word,
Just looked at me hard,
And then turned away,
She resented my presence from the first day,
When we got to the house where I was to stay,
My brown paper bag was snatched eagerly away,
I was taken up two flights of stairs to my room,
The attic they called it,
I didn't belong,
I knew I was being kept out of the way.

Abandoned and blamed

Every morning I went to school,
But only till noon because the school was so small,
There were to many children to all go together,
So the older children went after lunch,
I was in the same class as my new family's daughter,
But she rarely spoke,
And stayed with her friends,

Inspired By Love

She seemed to hate me,
But I didn't know why,
I was lonely and miserable most of the time,
But at least during school time my friends were around,
This helped a bit,
But when I went home,
I spent most of my time alone in my room,
All of my meals were eaten up there,
I could never be part of their family downstairs,
At church on Sundays I sat at the back,
I wasn't allowed to sit with them,
My birthday was marked by a letter from mum,
But to them it passed unnoticed,
The father was worse if he got in a mood,
I'd be locked in my room and given no food,
Whatever went wrong he'd blame it on me,
I didn't fit in so the fault was mine,
The mum was ok when he wasn't around,
But I think that she was scared of him too,
Every night the gas lamps were lit,
And blackouts put up at the windows,
I'd lay there alone awake in the darkness,
Wondering if mum blamed me for things too,
Was that why she had sent me away?
Crying into my pillow,
I would fitfully sleep.

Inspired By Love

<u>Hungry for home</u>

As Christmas approached,
Many friends went back home,
But mum said she'd rather I stayed,
Things back in London were getting worse,
And she didn't want me to get hurt,
So I stayed where I was,
And prayed every night that things where I was would improve,
But on Christmas day,
It was obvious they hadn't,
We had decorations and a small Christmas tree,
And although there was turkey for dinner,
I ate upstairs alone in my room,
As I had every day since I got there,
I did receive a parcel from mum,
With ribbons for my hair,
But their daughter got jealous,
So they were taken away,
And she wore them in her hair instead,
They told me she deserved them more,
Because a she was better behaved,
So I cried for the rest of that day,
But I managed to keep my new teddy bear,
I hid him under my bed,
I cried more and more as time went on,
Just longing to be at home with mum,

Inspired By Love

I needed a hug,
To see a kind smile,
For someone to say I was loved,
Then one day a letter arrived in the post,
With a message for me from mum,
My father was missing they didn't know where,
And our house was no longer there,
She had moved from London,
And had a house up north,
In the country so we would be safe,
She would send for me as soon as she could,
But that wouldn't be like home,
My world had been turned upside down once again.

A new home
The journey was long,
And I was afraid,
I didn't know what to expect,
Seeing mum was great,
But it wasn't the same,
After dad died everything changed,
I missed him so much and often cried,
And mum didn't laugh anymore,
Was it all my fault for going away?

Inspired By Love

I asked myself often each day,
The War had changed everything,
Nothing I knew remained,
I really missed London,
And all my friends,
And school had been worse than I'd feared,
The children had all got their own friends to play with,
They didn't even notice I was there,
When the teacher was talking,
I struggled a lot,
To understand what she was saying,
Her accent was different to what I'd been used to,
And nothing sounded the same,
The new house was nice,
And we had thatch,
Which was what straw on the roof was called,
But it wasn't like home,
And life was hard,
Food was still being rationed,
I found it hard to settle in and adjust to a new life there,

With things as they were I wondered a lot?
Would I ever be happy again?

Social Issues

Inspired By Love

Changing Times

We live in a time of constant change,
Always striving to stay up to date,
Even the familiar is becoming quite strange,
No wonder as people we are in such a state.

Always striving to stay up to date,
With the latest technology, fashion and trend,
No wonder as people we are in such a state,
What's wrong with the saying 'Make do and mend'?

With the latest technology, fashion and trend,
So many in debt as in loans they believe,
What's wrong with the saying 'make do and mend'?
If we work together, we could really achieve.

So many in debt as in loans they believe,
Let's make a difference, beginning today,
If we work together, we could really achieve,
Let's show all the world there's a far better way.

Inspired By Love

Let's make a difference, beginning today,
Even the familiar is becoming quite strange,
Let's show all the world there's a far better way,
We live in a time of constant change.

The purpose of waiting

Sitting and waiting,
Waiting for what,
Or for whom?
For something to happen,
Or someone to come?

Lord you are waiting,
For me to be ready,
For me to be willing,
To serve you in thought,
In word and in deed.

Lord you are watching,
The hearts of Your children,
Longing and aching,
For Your Church to respond,
Willing us to do Your will.

Inspired By Love

So while I wait,
Lord I will listen,
To what you are calling me to do,
And how I can serve you,
My whole life through.

What life means to me

We often take for granted all the luxuries of life,
We hardly ever stop to think what it is that really counts,
Do we really need all the man-made things we own?
Or do you think that we could live with natural things instead;

We simply don't appreciate until we are without,
The things which money cannot buy such as long life, health and love,
Valuables we cannot buy or replace when lost,
It's these that fill our lives so full of joy and wealth and fun;

Inspired By Love

It's at a time when we ourselves or someone that we love,
May suffer harm or injury or lose their life completely,
Then we may learn that money isn't all we need,
Its friendship and support which really count in times like these;

You cannot buy true friendship, but you can't live without it,
It's often easy to make friends, be yourself and don't pretend,
If you want a friends support also give them yours,
You need to be prepared to give if you are to receive;

If your life is to be complete a balance must be made,
We do need man-made things to enable us to live our life,
But without natures forces we would not survive,
Let's start from here and build anew, a balanced path to tread.

Inspired By Love

Our world

What can we see if we take the time?
To look around and ponder,
A world of beauty unblemished and pure?
Or torn apart by trouble and war?
Do we ever stop and think, about the actions that we take,
Or how the words we use each day affect people that we meet.

All of us have got the power,
To change lives for the better,
The time is now,
To take a stand,
And hold firm to what is right.
Not leave it until tomorrow,
Or say `that's someone else's fight`.
Be bold and take a chance,
Ask `how can I bless another? `.
Now every time we help a neighbour,
Their world will be filled with wonder.

Inspired By Love

A forgotten world

Why do people nowadays appear just not to see?
The wildlife and natural things that surround both you and me,
There's the grandeur of the mountains,
The serene and blue-green sea,
The varied blooms,
The roaming beasts,
They're here for all to see;

Why do people nowadays appear just not to hear?
All the howling winds and thunderstorms and deafening waterfalls,
There's whispering amongst the trees,
All the bird song pure and clear,
The buzzing bees,
The howling wolf,
Let's listen and let's hear;

Inspired By Love

It's time for people nowadays just to stop and think,
The time is now, at once, today tomorrow will be to late,
If we don't save what we have now,
It will all be gone next year,
Let's not destroy,
Let's build and grow,
There's hope for all out there.

A perfect world

In a perfect world there would be no war,
There would be no need for weapons,
The armed forces would cease to exist,
All murder and mass killing would stop;

Prejudice would die, not the victims of it,
So all the worlds people could live in harmony;

In a perfect world race would not matter,
Colour would form no barriers,
All language blocks could be overcome,
Different religions would live as one;

Inspired By Love

Physical force would end and talking would start,
Friendship could exist between all the world's nations;

In a perfect world animals roam free,
People protect not slaughter them,
Animals would no longer perform,
Zoos exist only as sanctuaries;

The natural world would be paradise for all,
None of the living things would ever need to fear;

Peace, friendship, love and harmony could exist forever,
The beautiful, heavenly, sin-free world would be everlasting.

Inspired By Love

Caring for carers

Who cares for you while you care for them?
You know you must do it,
You can't let them down,
You know you must not abandon them now,
It's not their fault but they feel like a burden,
You're doing your best but you've had enough;

When you need an ear there's no-one to listen,
When you need a shoulder there's never one there,
When you need a back-up you're completely abandoned,
Caring for carers just doesn't exist;

Who cares for you while you care for them?
You know you love them,
And they've always loved you,
You know that you mustn't blame them for your heartache,
But you feel depressed, alone and angry,
Who can you turn to is anyone there?

Inspired By Love

The truth is there's no-one to care for the carers,
Caring for carers,
Nobody does,
No-one ever will.

Can't keep up

The world goes by at such a pace,
Allowing no time to appreciate,
Things of beauty and of grace;
The world goes by at such a pace,
Joining in society's rat-race,
Continually fearing being late;
The world goes by at such a pace,
Allowing no time to appreciate.

Passing Through

Passing through, just passing through,
This is all we ever do,
One day here, one day there,
Sometimes even faster than that.

Inspired By Love

Never really stopping,
We can't appreciate the new,
Missing many miracles given,
Waiting for me and for you.

Just yesterday while on the train,
A quirky house flew by,
The likes of which I'm certain,
We have not seen before.

Its mustard yellow colour,
And circular tower turrets,
It seemed a most peculiar place,
I really must explore.

This is not so many miles away,
From my own front door,
Oh, why have I not been awake?
And noticed it before.

A valuable lesson for all of us,
To keep our eyes wide open,
And not to turn away,
To miss out on seeing new sights today,
Means missing memories from tomorrow.

Inspired By Love

What Future?

The wild is beautiful and nurtures life,
But Man's love is money and power to succeed,
Never to consider consequence of action,
Is a dangerous game to play.

The life of the fragile,
Of our very planet,
Rests in our own hands,
The futures of generations to come,
Dependant on us today.
If we truly want to build,
Give a better future to all,
Then we need to work together,
With nature and each other,
Not destroy, DESTROY, **DESTROY.**

Life cannot be bought with money,
And power doesn't't count,
But with thought for others,
With love and care,
Life can continue to flourish.

Inspired By Love

<u>Are We Truly Open?</u>

The church is the House of God,
We are His chosen people,
But are we open to His calling?
Are we truly open to all?

The church is the family of God,
We are called to be salt and light,
But do we really welcome and accept?
Do we love with the Heart of God?

The family of God should be open,
Open to all who believe,
But are we still guilty of building walls?
Do we still close the door in fear?

If someone arrives who is different,
Do we welcome them readily in?
Or are we still guilty of turning our backs,
And shunning the stranger who knocks?
Lord, help us be willing and open,
To receive anyone whom You send,
Melt our cold hearts to accept,
Those who are searching and need to belong.

Inspired By Love

Churches should grow and flourish,
Your family love, care and cherish,
Break down the barriers our hatred has built,
Pour Your light into darkness and fear.

Only then can we be truly open,
And serve You, united in love,
Help us to truly be Your church,
Accepting, forgiving and great.

Pastimes, People and Tributes

Inspired By Love

Pastimes

When I have some time to spare
I often read a book,
Or food with friends is nice to share,
I sometimes like to cook.

I sit and stitch a picture,
Or maybe make a card,
My leisure is such a mixture
Of simple things and hard.

One day I might chose to knit
And crochet on the next,
I pick it up and do a bit
Before I write some text.

Music has its role to play
A song can cheer your heart,
My hobbies vary each new day,
And quiz nights play their part.

Films I sometimes like to watch,
Or go and see a show,
At other times I sit and sketch
And poetry may flow.

Inspired By Love

If what I do brings pleasure
To people that I know,
It means, what I do for leisure
Will really make me glow.

<u>To Draw With Words</u>

I am not used to draw an image,
But to draw a picture in your mind,
By weaving different words together,
I enable your imagination to form pictures
unique to you.
I am therefore, not pencil or charcoal,
Nor pastels or paint,
I am a pen that draws using words,
Cleverly conjuring up images,
Different for each person,
But still providing fulfilment and joy.

Inspired By Love

Don't Lose Touch

We all arrived there nervously,
The place we were to meet at,
A few already knew each other,
But most of us knew no-one;

We said hello when we first met,
For a while that's how it stayed,
Just a brief hello each time we met,
But this was soon to alter;

As time went on we felt less shy,
Then we began to chatter,
We found we had some things in common,
Our friendship began to grow;

By the time the week had arrived,
The week of the performance,
We had a friendship warm and happy,
The fun we had was greater;

It's time for us to say goodbye,
But this need not be final,
Let's keep in touch with phone and letter,
And we'll soon meet up again.

Inspired By Love

The Audition

If you wish to be a part of any group or show,
An audition is the first step which you must undergo,
This is not an easy thing to do,
It causes me to shake,
The panel are just there to watch for one mistake;

After so much practice the audition day has come,
From this point on it's time to trust in memory and tongue,
You want your voice to be at its best,
You're waiting for your turn,
You now begin to wonder whether this is what you yearn;

At last your name is called and you walk onto the stage,
Those fifteen minutes seem to be an everlasting age,
You have done your song and dialogue,
You then go through some dance,
Now that it's all over you feel you're in a trance;

Inspired By Love

Finally the waiting's over, is it yes or no?
You feel your heart begin to pound and panic starts to flow,
It is your turn now to hear the news,
A feeling of relief,
Although you've passed it's now that all the hard work starts.

A Trip to the Theatre

A pleasant summer evening,
Tranquil and serene,
Romance and drama combining
In tonight's Shakespearian play.
Performed in the grounds of a castle,
The sun setting all around
Open air
Theatre is unique, and
Has a special charm.
Everyone just soaking up
The atmosphere that surrounds, when
Here come the actors onto the stage,
Excited chatter fades.
All are spellbound as in
Time the story will unfold,
Recapturing a time long before, through
Enchanting music and lyrical speech not used in life today.

Inspired By Love

Can You Feel the Music?

Music brings such joy to expectant ears,
Each tune and all its harmonies combine,
Printed pages brought to life through the years,
Sometimes played as background while people dine.
Emotions can be stirred, both yours and mine,
Expressing love and faithfulness in song,
When put to music words can be divine,
Enjoyed by one alone or by a throng,
Music can unite us and help all to belong.

Music

Music brings a joy,
Lifting our spirits and hearts,
Brightening the day,
Despite the cold wind and grey,
A song can bring a warm glow.

Inspired By Love

What Can I Hear?

Tall grasses dancing,
At a distance church bells ring,
Traffics constant hum.

What Can I See?

The dampness of dew,
Variations of each hue,
Folks passing chatter.

The Character of a Creator

In 1866 a little girl was born,
Whose love and passion for wildlife,
Would bring joy to generations,
Through her art and through her tales,
Animal characters were born,
Simple picture letters sent to the son of a friend,
Were just the humble beginnings,
Of what was to be her life's work,
In 1905 she bought Hilltop House,
And this became her home,
Celebrated in the tale of a mouse,

Inspired By Love

Given the name of Samuel Whiskers,
Having lost her first love,
She escaped into the hills,
And having found love for a second time,
Married in 1913,
She'd always loved the Lake District,
And was determined it stay unspoilt,
Her thirty years of married life,
Was spent promoting this cause,
As well as writing books and breeding
Hardwick sheep,
At the end of 1943,
She lost her fight for life,
But she'll never be forgotten,
The remarkable Beatrix Potter.

Diana - A Perfect Princess
Princess of Our Hearts, Queen of Us All

A serene and lovely person,
Unselfish, true and loyal,
She never would condemn or turn her back
on me or you,
No-one was to humble,
Her life was filled so full,
Of positive and worthy things,

Inspired By Love

Diana lived and loved,
A princess of the people,
Forever cherished in our hearts;
The great big void left by your loss,
This world will never forget,
A radiant star lost from heaven not to be replaced,
Those people that you touched,
In work or word or deed,
Never will forget their princess,
You changed their life for good,
Those memories will live on,
Goodbye to a perfect princess;
Thank you for your life of service,
Now perfect, positive, peaceful princess,
Diana, rest in peace.

Tribute to a Maid

A verse by William Wordsworth on a young girl's tomb,
Paying tribute to her character,
And homage to her life,
Comparing her to nature,
And radiating love,
Lord you must delight in such a pure and faithful heart.

Inspired By Love

Prayer for Margot

May our
Amazing
Redeemer
Graciously
Outpour His love
To you.

Anna's Message

She stands at the front alone and afraid,
A waif like figure with tears in her eyes,
``I had a dream last night``, she began,
Her trembling form looking so small,
``God gave me a picture of Him talking to me,
But I could not hear Him,
So many other voices were drowning him out,
I believe he wants me to listen more,
Listen to Him and not to the crowd,
Spend time alone in His presence,
Just me and my Lord,
And He told me to share this with you``,
This child of eleven returned to her seat,
But had delivered a message we all needed to hear,
A young prophetess named Anna.

Inspired By Love

<u>Nancy's Soliloquy</u>

Frowned on,
Looked down,
By people that I meet,
Judged by,
Accused by,
The toffs who pass me in the street,
Thieving from childhood just to survive,
Loving a man who can't love me back,
Trapped here forever without an escape;
I must help this kid,
He's been offered some hope,
Whatever it takes he must 'ave his chance,
Of a far better life,
Away from this crime and abuse,
People who love him and care for his needs,
Not bully's who are only filled with greed;
Whatever life throws at me,
I can cope,
To help this kid could cost me my life,
But I must know that I've done my best to save his,
I can't condemn him to live as I've lived,
So I'll take him tonight,
Out of the darkness,
Into the light,
He trusts me and I can't betray him,
But it must be done quickly,

Inspired By Love

And without any fuss,
Or his life's in danger as well as my own;
I must make the arrangements,
They'll just 'ave to trust me,
And believe what I say,
His new life must start,
And start today.

The Fountain of Knowledge

In a courtyard stands a fountain,
With a statue at its centre,
The boy clutches the bud of a water lily,
And his face looks dreamily skywards,
Just to know what he is thinking,
To have seen what he has seen,
From the fifties to the present day,
Events of tragedy and joy,
Have often passed him by,
Forgotten now,
Never to be known,
Lost to unremembered history.

Inspired By Love

Smugglers

Secret passages underground,
Meetings in the dark,
United in a common cause,
Guilty though they were.
Gentlemen with secret lives
Looking to secure,
Earnings and financial gain,
Running risks at every turn.
Smuggling was their game.

Living in Exile

Lost and a stranger,
Unwanted and fearful,
What will become of me?
How will I live?

I had a life I was happy with,
People I knew and who cared,
What now is next for me?
Will I survive?

Inspired By Love

Driven away by hatred and power,
Unable to stay, I had no protection,
Now I have what?
No hope and no home.

How long must I stay here?
Forever, or just for a while?
Will hope ever come back to me?
Will I ever again be free?

Alone I will stay,
For as long as it lasts,
But I long for a light,
Just once more to shine,
To shine so brightly,
So brightly for me alone.

Constants

Different faces,
Same warm welcome,
An ethos of love and family,
Constantly changing,
Moving on,
Yet God is the constant remaining.

Inspired By Love

Friendships are formed,
Hard to say goodbye,
But knowing a new brother or sister,
Waits just around the corner,
Welcoming someone new,
Another stranger,
Not for long,
Because God is the constant remaining.

The world is wide,
But not too wide,
Lives can be forever linked,
Because God is the constant remaining.

An Alien at Home

Returning to where I was born,
Hoping once more to belong,
But nothing remains that I know here now,
Not one single person even knows my name.
I should not be surprised,
So long has elapsed,
When I left I was but a child,
But I had been so happy here.
So, I vowed as I grew,

Inspired By Love

That one day I knew,
I must return and maybe remain?
No longer does that vow even seem real,
As I stand in utter despair.
An alien now,
Just another lost stranger,
In a place I had hoped to call home.

The Past is Not Your Future

Our lives are shaped by what has passed,
But we cannot let what we have suffered,
Destroy what is to come.
The past can shape our future,
But the harshest pain won't last.
We are not called to stay trapped and scared,
But to listen to the master.
Do not allow yourselves to dwell,
On what has passed away,
But take a step of faith today,
Trust and hope in the Lord,
For what is still to come.
Struggles and battles,
Sorrow and Pain,
Will still blight our daily lives,

Inspired By Love

But the Holy Dove will always guide us,
If we follow in His way.
In the end,
When we say prayers out loud,
Walls begin to tumble,
The Sovereign light at last gets in,
And every heart to love will come,
To worship Christ the King.

www.ingramcontent.com/pod-product-compliance
Lightning Source LLC
Chambersburg PA
CBHW071450040426
42444CB00008B/1275